Robert Louis Stevenson

The Complete Poetry

e-artnow 2018

Reading suggestions (available from e-artnow as Print & eBook)

Samuel Taylor Coleridge
The Complete Works of Samuel Taylor Coleridge: Poetry, Plays, Literary Essays, Lectures, Autobiography and Letters (Classic Illustrated Edition)

John Keats
Sonnets (Complete Edition)

John Keats
John Keats: Lamia (Unabridged Edition)

Robert Louis Stevenson
The Collected Memoirs, Travel Sketches and Island Literature

John Keats
The Eve of St. Agnes (Complete Edition)

Edwin Arnold
Collected Poetry of Edwin Arnold (With Original Illustrations): The Light of Asia, Light of the World or The Great Consummation (Christian Poem), The Indian Song of Songs, Oriental Poems, The Song Celestial or Bhagavad-Gita, Potiphar's Wife...

Robert Louis Stevenson
The Complete Poetry of Robert Louis Stevenson

Samuel Taylor Coleridge
The Complete Works: Poetry, Plays, Literary Essays, Lectures, Autobiography and Letters (Classic Illustrated Edition)

John Keats
The Complete Poetry of John Keats

George MacDonald
The Complete Poetry of George MacDonald

Robert Louis Stevenson

The Complete Poetry

Poems by a prolific Scottish writer, author of Treasure Island, The Strange Case of Dr. Jekyll and Mr. Hyde, Kidnapped, The Master of Ballantrae and A Child's Garden of Verses

e-artnow, 2018
Contact: info@e-artnow.org
ISBN 978-80-268-9103-1

Contents

BALLADS	15
THE SONG OF RAHÉRO: A LEGEND OF TAHITI	16
THE SLAYING OF TÁMATÉA	17
THE VENGING OF TÁMATÉA	21
RAHÉRO	26
THE FEAST OF FAMINE MARQUESAN MANNERS	30
THE PRIEST'S VIGIL	30
THE LOVERS	32
THE FEAST	34
THE RAID	37
TICONDEROGA A LEGEND OF THE WEST HIGHLANDS	39
TICONDEROGA	39
THE SAYING OF THE NAME	40
THE SEEKING OF THE NAME	43
THE PLACE OF THE NAME	45
HEATHER ALE	47
CHRISTMAS AT SEA	49
A CHILD'S GARDEN OF VERSES	51
TO ALISON CUNNINGHAM	52
BED IN SUMMER	54
A THOUGHT	56
AT THE SEA-SIDE	59
YOUNG NIGHT-THOUGHT	61
WHOLE DUTY OF CHILDREN	62
RAIN	63
PIRATE STORY	65
FOREIGN LANDS	66
WINDY NIGHTS	69
TRAVEL	70
SINGING	73
LOOKING FORWARD	74
A GOOD PLAY	75
WHERE GO THE BOATS?	76
AUNTIE'S SKIRTS	78
THE LAND OF COUNTERPANE	79
THE LAND OF NOD	80
MY SHADOW	82
SYSTEM	84

A GOOD BOY	85
ESCAPE AT BEDTIME	86
MARCHING SONG	88
THE COW	89
HAPPY THOUGHT	90
THE WIND	91
KEEPSAKE MILL	92
GOOD AND BAD CHILDREN	94
FOREIGN CHILDREN	95
THE SUN TRAVELS	97
THE LAMPLIGHTER	98
MY BED IS A BOAT	100
THE MOON	101
THE SWING	102
TIME TO RISE	103
LOOKING-GLASS RIVER	104
FAIRY BREAD	105
FROM A RAILWAY CARRIAGE	106
WINTER-TIME	107
THE HAYLOFT	109
FAREWELL TO THE FARM	111
NORTHWEST PASSAGE	112
THE CHILD ALONE	115
MY SHIP AND I	118
MY KINGDOM	119
PICTURE-BOOKS IN WINTER	120
MY TREASURES	122
BLOCK CITY	123
THE LAND OF STORYBOOKS	124
ARMIES IN THE FIRE	125
THE LITTLE LAND	126
GARDEN DAYS	129
NEST EGGS	132
THE FLOWERS	134
SUMMER SUN	136
THE DUMB SOLDIER	137
AUTUMN FIRES	139
THE GARDENER	140
HISTORICAL ASSOCIATIONS	141
ENVOYS	142

TO MY MOTHER	144
TO AUNTIE	145
TO MINNIE	147
TO MY NAME-CHILD	149
TO ANY READER	151
UNDERWOODS	153
DEDICATION	155
BOOK I	157
ENVOY	159
A SONG OF THE ROAD	160
THE CANOE SPEAKS	161
THE HOUSE BEAUTIFUL	163
A VISIT FROM THE SEA	164
TO A GARDENER	165
TO MINNIE	166
TO K. de M.	167
TO N. V. de G. S.	168
TO WILL. H. LOW	169
TO MRS. WILL. H. LOW	170
TO H. F. BROWN	171
TO ANDREW LANG	172
ET TU IN ARCADIA VIXISTI	173
TO W.E. HENLEY	175
HENRY JAMES	176
THE MIRROR SPEAKS	177
KATHARINE	178
TO F. J. S.	179
REQUIEM	180
THE CELESTIAL SURGEON	181
OUR LADY OF THE SNOWS	182
THE SICK CHILD	186
IN MEMORIAM F.A.S.	187
TO MY FATHER	188
IN THE STATES	189
A PORTRAIT	190
A CAMP	191
THE COUNTRY OF THE CAMISARDS	192
SKERRYVORE	193
SKERRYVORE THE PARALLEL	194
BOOK II	197

TABLE OF COMMON SCOTTISH VOWEL SOUNDS	199
THE MAKER TO POSTERITY	200
ILLE TERRARUM	201
A MILE AN' A BITTOCK	203
A LOWDEN SABBATH MORN	204
THE SPAEWIFE	207
THE BLAST —	208
THE COUNTERBLAST —	209
THE COUNTERBLAST IRONICAL	211
THEIR LAUREATE TO AN ACADEMY CLASS	212
EMBRO HIE KIRK	214
THE SCOTSMAN'S RETURN FROM ABROAD	216
MY CONSCIENCE!	220
TO DOCTOR JOHN BROWN	221
SONGS OF TRAVEL	223
THE VAGABOND	225
YOUTH AND LOVE — I	227
YOUTH AND LOVE — II	229
WE HAVE LOVED OF YORE	233
MATER TRIUMPHANS	235
TO THE TUNE OF WANDERING WILLIE	237
WINTER	239
TO DR. HAKE	241
TO ——	243
IF THIS WERE FAITH	245
MY WIFE	247
TO THE MUSE	249
TO AN ISLAND PRINCESS	251
TO KALAKAUA	253
TO PRINCESS KAIULANI	255
TO MOTHER MARYANNE	257
IN MEMORIAM E.H.	259
TO MY WIFE	261
TO MY OLD FAMILIARS	263
TO S. C.	265
THE HOUSE OF TEMBINOKA	267
THE SONG	269
THE WOODMAN	273
TROPIC RAIN	277
AN END OF TRAVEL	279

TO S.R. CROCKETT	281
EVENSONG	283
THE LESSON OF THE MASTER	285
A FAMILIAR EPISTLE	287
EPISTLE TO CHARLES BAXTER	289
EPISTLE TO ALBERT DEW-SMITH	291
RONDELS	293
OF HIS PITIABLE TRANSFORMATION	295
THE SUSQUEHANNAH AND THE DELAWARE	297
ALCAICS TO HORATIO F. BROWN	299
A LYTLE JAPE OF TUSHERIE	301
TO VIRGIL AND DORA WILLIAMS	303
BURLESQUE SONNET	305
THE FINE PACIFIC ISLANDS	307
AULD REEKIE	309
THE CONSECRATION OF BRAILLE	311
SONG	313
THE LIGHTKEEPER	315

BALLADS

THE SONG OF RAHÉRO: A LEGEND OF TAHITI

TO
ORI A ORI

Ori, my brother in the island mode,
In every tongue and meaning much my friend,
This story of your country and your clan,
In your loved house, your too much honoured guest,
I made in English. Take it, being done;

And let me sign it with the name you gave.
TERIITERA.

I

THE SLAYING OF TÁMATÉA

It fell in the days of old, as the men of Taiárapu tell,
A youth went forth to the fishing, and fortune favoured him well.
Támatéa his name: gullible, simple, and kind.
Comely of countenance, nimble of body, empty of mind,
His mother ruled him and loved him beyond the wont of a wife,
Serving the lad for eyes and living herself in his life.
Alone from the sea and the fishing came Támatéa the fair,
Urging his boat to the beach, and the mother awaited him there.
— "Long may you live!" said she. "Your fishing has sped to a wish.
And now let us choose for the king the fairest of all your fish.
For fear inhabits the palace and grudging grows in the land,
Marked is the sluggardly foot and marked the niggardly hand,
The hours and the miles are counted, the tributes numbered and weighed,
And woe to him that comes short, and woe to him that delayed!"

So spoke on the beach the mother, and counselled the wiser thing.
For Rahéro stirred in the country and secretly mined the king.
Nor were the signals wanting of how the leaven wrought,
In the cords of obedience loosed and the tributes grudgingly brought.
And when last to the temple of Oro the boat with the victim sped,
And the priest uncovered the basket and looked on the face of the dead,
Trembling fell upon all at sight of an ominous thing,
For there was the aito dead, and he of the house of the king.
So spake on the beach the mother, matter worthy of note,
And wattled a basket well, and chose a fish from the boat;
And Támatéa the pliable shouldered the basket and went,
And travelled, and sang as he travelled, a lad that was well content.
Still the way of his going was round by the roaring coast,
Where the ring of the reef is broke and the trades run riot the most.
On his left, with smoke as of battle, the billows battered the land;
Unscalable, turreted mountains rose on the inner hand.
And cape, and village, and river, and vale, and mountain above,
Each had a name in the land for men to remember and love;
And never the name of a place, but lo! a song in its praise:
Ancient and unforgotten, songs of the earlier days
That the elders taught to the young, and at night, in the full of the moon,
Garlanded boys and maidens sang together in tune.

Támatéa the placable went with a lingering foot;
He sang as loud as a bird, he whistled hoarse as a flute;
He broiled in the sun, he breathed in the grateful shadow of trees,
In the icy stream of the rivers he waded over the knees;
And still in his empty mind crowded, a thousandfold,
The deeds of the strong and the songs of the cunning heroes of old.
And now was he come to a place Taiárapu honoured the most,
Where a silent valley of woods debouched on the noisy coast,
Spewing a level river. There was a haunt of Pai.
There, in his potent youth, when his parents drove him to die,
Honoura lived like a beast, lacking the lamp and the fire,
Washed by the rains of the trade and clotting his hair in the mire;

And there, so mighty his hands, he bent the tree to his foot —
So keen the spur of his hunger, he plucked it naked of fruit.
There, as she pondered the clouds for the shadow of coming ills,
Ahupu, the woman of song, walked on high on the hills.
Of these was Rahéro sprung, a man of a godly race;
And inherited cunning of spirit, and beauty of body and face.
Of yore in his youth, as an aito, Rahéro wandered the land,
Delighting maids with his tongue, smiting men with his hand.
Famous he was in his youth; but before the midst of his life
Paused, and fashioned a song of farewell to glory and strife.

House of mine (it went), *house upon the sea,*
Belov'd of all my fathers, more belov'd by me!
Vale of the strong Honoura, deep ravine of Pai,
Again in your woody summits I hear the trade-wind cry.
House of mine, in your walls, strong sounds the sea,
Of all sounds on earth, dearest sound to me.
I have heard the applause of men, I have heard it arise and die:
Sweeter now in my house I hear the trade-wind cry.

These were the words of his singing, other the thought of his heart;
For secret desire of glory vexed him, dwelling apart.
Lazy and crafty he was, and loved to lie in the sun,
And loved the cackle of talk and the true word uttered in fun;
Lazy he was, his roof was ragged, his table was lean,
And the fish swam safe in his sea, and he gathered the near and the green.
He sat in his house and laughed, but he loathed the king of the land,
And he uttered the grudging word under the covering hand.
Treason spread from his door; and he looked for a day to come,
A day of the crowding people, a day of the summoning drum,
When the vote should be taken, the king be driven forth in disgrace,
And Rahéro, the laughing and lazy, sit and rule in his place.
Here Támatéa came, and beheld the house on the brook;
And Rahéro was there by the way and covered an oven to cook.

Naked he was to the loins, but the tattoo covered the lack,
And the sun and the shadow of palms dappled his muscular back.
Swiftly he lifted his head at the fall of the coming feet,
And the water sprang in his mouth with a sudden desire of meat:
For he marked the basket carried, covered from flies and the sun;
And Rahéro buried his fire, but the meat in his house was done.
Forth he stepped; and took, and delayed the boy, by the hand;
And vaunted the joys of meat and the ancient ways of the land:
— "Our sires of old in Taiárapu, they that created the race,
Ate ever with eager hand, nor regarded season or place,
Ate in the boat at the oar, on the way afoot; and at night
Arose in the midst of dreams to rummage the house for a bite.
It is good for the youth in his turn to follow the way of the sire;
And behold how fitting the time! for here do I cover my fire."
— "I see the fire for the cooking, but never the meat to cook,"
Said Támatéa. — "Tut!" said Rahéro. "Here in the brook,
And there in the tumbling sea, the fishes are thick as flies,
Hungry like healthy men, and like pigs for savour and size:
Crayfish crowding the river, sea-fish thronging the sea."
— "Well, it may be," says the other, "and yet be nothing to me.

Fain would I eat, but alas! I have needful matter in hand,
Since I carry my tribute of fish to the jealous king of the land."
Now at the word a light sprang in Rahéro's eyes.
"I will gain me a dinner," thought he, "and lend the king a surprise."
And he took the lad by the arm, as they stood by the side of the track,
And smiled, and rallied, and flattered, and pushed him forward and back.
It was "You that sing like a bird, I never have heard you sing,"
And "The lads when I was a lad were none so feared of a king.
And of what account is an hour, when the heart is empty of guile?
But come, and sit in the house and laugh with the women awhile;
And I will but drop my hook, and behold! the dinner made."
So Támatéa the pliable hung up his fish in the shade
On a tree by the side of the way; and Rahéro carried him in,
Smiling as smiles the fowler when flutters the bird to the gin,
And chose him a shining hook, and viewed it with sedulous eye,
And breathed and burnished it well on the brawn of his naked thigh,
And set a mat for the gull, and bade him be merry and bide,
Like a man concerned for his guest, and the fishing, and nothing beside.
Now when Rahéro was forth, he paused and hearkened, and heard
The gull jest in the house and the women laugh at his word;

And stealthily crossed to the side of the way, to the shady place
Where the basket hung on a mango; and craft transfigured his face.
Deftly he opened the basket, and took of the fat of the fish,
The cut of kings and chieftains, enough for a goodly dish.
This he wrapped in a leaf, set on the fire to cook,
And buried; and next the marred remains of the tribute he took,
And doubled and packed them well, and covered the basket close.
— "There is a buffet, my king," quoth he, "and a nauseous dose!" —
And hung the basket again in the shade, in a cloud of flies;
— "And there is a sauce to your dinner, king of the crafty eyes!"
Soon as the oven was open, the fish smelt excellent good.
In the shade, by the house of Rahéro, down they sat to their food,
And cleared the leaves, in silence, or uttered a jest and laughed
And raising the cocoanut bowls, buried their faces and quaffed.
But chiefly in silence they ate; and soon as the meal was done,
Rahéro feigned to remember and measured the hour by the sun
And "Támatéa," quoth he, "it is time to be jogging, my lad."
So Támatéa arose, doing ever the thing he was bade,
And carelessly shouldered the basket, and kindly saluted his host;
And again the way of his going was round by the roaring coast.

Long he went; and at length was aware of a pleasant green,
And the stems and shadows of palms, and roofs of lodges between.
There sate, in the door of his palace, the king on a kingly seat,
And aitos stood armed around, and the yottowas sat at his feet.
But fear was a worm in his heart: fear darted his eyes;
And he probed men's faces for treasons and pondered their speech for lies.
To him came Támatéa, the basket slung in his hand,
And paid him the due obeisance standing as vassals stand.
In silence hearkened the king, and closed the eyes in his face,
Harbouring odious thoughts and the baseless fears of the base;
In silence accepted the gift and sent the giver away.

So Támatéa departed, turning his back on the day.
And lo! as the king sat brooding, a rumour rose in the crowd;
The yottowas nudged and whispered, the commons murmured aloud;
Tittering fell upon all at sight of the impudent thing,
At the sight of a gift unroyal flung in the face of a king.
And the face of the king turned white and red with anger and shame
In their midst; and the heart in his body was water and then was flame;
Till of a sudden, turning, he gripped an aito hard,
A youth that stood with his ómare, one of the daily guard,
And spat in his ear a command, and pointed and uttered a name,
And hid in the shade of the house his impotent anger and shame.

Now Támatéa the fool was far on his homeward way,
The rising night in his face, behind him the dying day.
Rahéro saw him go by, and the heart of Rahéro was glad,
Devising shame to the king and nowise harm to the lad;
And all that dwelt by the way saw and saluted him well,
For he had the face of a friend and the news of the town to tell;
And pleased with the notice of folk, and pleased that his journey was done,
Támatéa drew homeward, turning his back to the sun.
And now was the hour of the bath in Taiárapu: far and near
The lovely laughter of bathers rose and delighted his ear.
Night massed in the valleys; the sun on the mountain coast
Struck, endlong; and above the clouds embattled their host,
And glowed and gloomed on the heights; and the heads of the palms were gems,
And far to the rising eve extended the shade of their stems;
And the shadow of Támatéa hovered already at home.
And sudden the sound of one coming and running light as the foam
Struck on his ear; and he turned, and lo! a man on his track,
Girded and armed with an ómare, following hard at his back.
At a bound the man was upon him; — and, or ever a word was said,
The loaded end of the ómare fell and laid him dead.

II

THE VENGING OF TÁMATÉA

Thus was Rahéro's treason; thus and no further it sped.
The king sat safe in his place and a kindly fool was dead.
But the mother of Támatéa arose with death in her eyes.
All night long, and the next, Taiárapu rang with her cries.
As when a babe in the wood turns with a chill of doubt
And perceives nor home, nor friends, for the trees have closed her about,
The mountain rings and her breast is torn with the voice of despair:
So the lion-like woman idly wearied the air
For a while, and pierced men's hearing in vain, and wounded their hearts.
But as when the weather changes at sea, in dangerous parts,
And sudden the hurricane wrack unrolls up the front of the sky,
At once the ship lies idle, the sails hang silent on high,
The breath of the wind that blew is blown out like the flame of a lamp,
And the silent armies of death draw near with inaudible tramp:
So sudden, the voice of her weeping ceased; in silence she rose
And passed from the house of her sorrow, a woman clothed with repose,
Carrying death in her breast and sharpening death in her hand.
Hither she went and thither in all the coasts of the land.
They tell that she feared not to slumber alone, in the dead of night,
In accursed places; beheld, unblenched, the ribbon of light

Spin from temple to temple; guided the perilous skiff,
Abhorred not the paths of the mountain and trod the verge of the cliff;
From end to end of the island, thought not the distance long,
But forth from king to king carried the tale of her wrong.
To king after king, as they sat in the palace door, she came,
Claiming kinship, declaiming verses, naming her name
And the names of all of her fathers; and still, with a heart on the rack,
Jested to capture a hearing and laughed when they jested back;
So would deceive them a while, and change and return in a breath,
And on all the men of Vaiau imprecate instant death;
And tempt her kings — for Vaiau was a rich and prosperous land,
And flatter — for who would attempt it but warriors mighty of hand?
And change in a breath again and rise in a strain of song,
Invoking the beaten drums, beholding the fall of the strong,
Calling the fowls of the air to come and feast on the dead.
And they held the chin in silence, and heard her, and shook the head;
For they knew the men of Taiárapu famous in battle and feast,
Marvellous eaters and smiters: the men of Vaiau not least.
To the land of the Námunu-úra, to Paea, at length she came,
To men who were foes to the Tevas and hated their race and name.
There was she well received, and spoke with Hiopa the king.
And Hiopa listened, and weighed, and wisely considered the thing.
"Here in the back of the isle we dwell in a sheltered place,"
Quoth he to the woman, "in quiet, a weak and peaceable race.
But far in the teeth of the wind lofty Taiárapu lies;
Strong blows the wind of the trade on its seaward face, and cries
Aloud in the top of arduous mountains, and utters its song
In green continuous forests. Strong is the wind, and strong

And fruitful and hardy the race, famous in battle and feast,
Marvellous eaters and smiters: the men of Vaiau not least.
Now hearken to me, my daughter, and hear a word of the wise:
How a strength goes linked with a weakness, two by two, like the eyes.
They can wield the ómare well and cast the javelin far;
Yet are they greedy and weak as the swine and the children are.
Plant we, then, here at Paea a garden of excellent fruits;
Plant we bananas and kava and taro, the king of roots;
Let the pigs in Paea be tapu and no man fish for a year;
And of all the meat in Tahiti gather we threefold here.
So shall the fame of our plenty fill the island and so,
At last, on the tongue of rumour, go where we wish it to go.
Then shall the pigs of Taiárapu raise their snouts in the air;
But we sit quiet and wait, as the fowler sits by the snare,
And tranquilly fold our hands, till the pigs come nosing the food:
But meanwhile build us a house of Trotéa, the stubborn wood,

Bind it with incombustible thongs, set a roof to the room,
Too strong for the hands of a man to dissever or fire to consume;
And there, when the pigs come trotting, there shall the feast be spread,
There shall the eye of the morn enlighten the feasters dead.
So be it done; for I have a heart that pities your state,
And Nateva and Námunu-úra are fire and water for hate."
All was done as he said, and the gardens prospered; and now
The fame of their plenty went out, and word of it came to Vaiau.
For the men of Námunu-úra sailed, to the windward far,
Lay in the offing by south where the towns of the Tevas are,
And cast overboard of their plenty; and lo! at the Tevas' feet
The surf on all the beaches tumbled treasures of meat.
In the salt of the sea, a harvest tossed with the refluent foam;
And the children gleaned it in playing, and ate and carried it home;
And the elders stared and debated, and wondered and passed the jest,
But whenever a guest came by eagerly questioned the guest;
And little by little, from one to another, the word went round:
"In all the borders of Paea the victual rots on the ground,
And swine are plenty as rats. And now, when they fare to the sea,
The men of the Námunu-úra glean from under the tree
And load the canoe to the gunwale with all that is toothsome to eat;
And all day long on the sea the jaws are crushing the meat,

The steersman eats at the helm, the rowers munch at the oar,
And at length, when their bellies are full, overboard with the store!"
Now was the word made true, and soon as the bait was bare,
All the pigs of Taiárapu raised their snouts in the air.
Songs were recited, and kinship was counted, and tales were told
How war had severed of late but peace had cemented of old
The clans of the island. "To war," said they, "now set we an end,
And hie to the Námunu-úra even as a friend to a friend."
So judged, and a day was named; and soon as the morning broke,
Canoes were thrust in the sea, and the houses emptied of folk.
Strong blew the wind of the south, the wind that gathers the clan;
Along all the line of the reef the clamorous surges ran;
And the clouds were piled on the top of the island mountain-high,
A mountain throned on a mountain. The fleet of canoes swept by

In the midst, on the green lagoon, with a crew released from care,
Sailing an even water, breathing a summer air,
Cheered by a cloudless sun; and ever to left and right,
Bursting surge on the reef, drenching storms on the height.
So the folk of Vaiau sailed and were glad all day,
Coasting the palm-tree cape and crossing the populous bay
By all the towns of the Tevas; and still as they bowled along,
Boat would answer to boat with jest and laughter and song,

And the people of all the towns trooped to the sides of the sea,
And gazed from under the hand or sprang aloft on the tree
Hailing and cheering. Time failed them for more to do;
The holiday village careened to the wind, and was gone from view
Swift as a passing bird; and ever as onward it bore,
Like the cry of the passing bird, bequeathed its song to the shore —
Desirable laughter of maids and the cry of delight of the child.
And the gazer, left behind, stared at the wake and smiled.
By all the towns of the Tevas they went, and Pápara last,
The home of the chief, the place of muster in war; and passed
The march of the lands of the clan, to the lands of an alien folk.
And there, from the dusk of the shoreside palms, a column of smoke
Mounted and wavered and died in the gold of the setting sun,
"Paea!" they cried. "It is Paea." And so was the voyage done.
In the early fall of the night Hiopa came to the shore,
And beheld and counted the comers, and lo, they were forty score;
The pelting feet of the babes that ran already and played,
The clean-lipped smile of the boy, the slender breasts of the maid,
And mighty limbs of women, stalwart mothers of men.
The sires stood forth unabashed; but a little back from his ken

Clustered the scarcely nubile, the lads and maids, in a ring,
Fain of each other, afraid of themselves, aware of the king
And aping behaviour, but clinging together with hands and eyes,
With looks that were kind like kisses, and laughter tender as sighs.
There, too, the grandsire stood, raising his silver crest,
And the impotent hands of a suckling groped in his barren breast.
The childhood of love, the pair well married, the innocent brood,
The tale of the generations repeated and ever renewed —
Hiopa beheld them together, all the ages of man,
And a moment shook in his purpose.
But these were the foes of his clan,
And he trod upon pity, and came, and civilly greeted the king,
And gravely entreated Rahéro; and for all that could fight or sing,
And claimed a name in the land, had fitting phrases of praise:
But with all who were well-descended he spoke of the ancient days.
And "'Tis true," said he, "that in Paea the victual rots on the ground;
But, friends, your number is many; and pigs must be hunted and found,
And the lads must troop to the mountains to bring the féis down,
And around the bowls of the kava cluster the maids of the town.
So, for tonight, sleep here; but king, common, and priest
Tomorrow, in order due, shall sit with me in the feast."

Sleepless the livelong night, Hiopa's followers toiled.
The pigs screamed and were slaughtered; the spars of the guest-house oiled,

The leaves spread on the floor. In many a mountain glen
The moon drew shadows of trees on the naked bodies of men
Plucking and bearing fruits; and in all the bounds of the town
Red glowed the cocoanut fires, and were buried and trodden down.
Thus did seven of the yottowas toil with their tale of the clan,
But the eighth wrought with his lads, hid from the sight of man.
In the deeps of the woods they laboured, piling the fuel high
In fagots, the load of a man, fuel seasoned and dry,
Thirsty to seize upon fire and apt to blurt into flame.
And now was the day of the feast. The forests, as morning came,
Tossed in the wind, and the peaks quaked in the blaze of the day —
And the cocoanuts showered on the ground, rebounding and rolling away:
A glorious morn for a feast, a famous wind for a fire.
To the hall of feasting Hiopa led them, mother and sire
And maid and babe in a tale, the whole of the holiday throng.
Smiling they came, garlanded green, not dreaming of wrong;
And for every three, a pig, tenderly cooked in the ground,
Waited; and féi, the staff of life, heaped in a mound
For each where he sat; — for each, bananas roasted and raw
Piled with a bountiful hand, as for horses hay and straw
Are stacked in a stable; and fish, the food of desire,

And plentiful vessels of sauce, and breadfruit gilt in the fire; —
And kava was common as water. Feasts have there been ere now,
And many, but never a feast like that of the folk of Vaiau.
All day long they ate with the resolute greed of brutes,
And turned from the pigs to the fish, and again from the fish to the fruits,
And emptied the vessels of sauce, and drank of the kava deep;
Till the young lay stupid as stones, and the strongest nodded to sleep.
Sleep that was mighty as death and blind as a moonless night
Tethered them hand and foot; and their souls were drowned, and the light
Was cloaked from their eyes. Senseless together, the old and the young,
The fighter deadly to smite and the prater cunning of tongue,
The woman wedded and fruitful, inured to the pangs of birth,
And the maid that knew not of kisses, blindly sprawled on the earth.
From the hall Hiopa the king and his chiefs came stealthily forth.
Already the sun hung low and enlightened the peaks of the north;
But the wind was stubborn to die and blew as it blows at morn,
Showering the nuts in the dusk, and e'en as a banner is torn,
High on the peaks of the island, shattered the mountain cloud.
And now at once, at a signal, a silent, emulous crowd

Set hands to the work of death, hurrying to and fro,
Like ants, to furnish the fagots, building them broad and low,
And piling them high and higher around the walls of the hall.
Silence persisted within, for sleep lay heavy on all
But the mother of Támatéa stood at Hiopa's side,
And shook for terror and joy like a girl that is a bride,
Night fell on the toilers, and first Hiopa the wise
Made the round of the hose, visiting all with his eyes;
And all was piled to the eaves, and fuel blockaded the door;
And within, in the house beleaguered, slumbered the forty score.
Then was an aito despatched and came with fire in his hand,
And Hiopa took it. — "Within," said he, "is the life of a land;

And behold! I breathe on the coal, I breathe on the dales of the east,
And silence falls on forest and shore; the voice of the feast
Is quenched, and the smoke of cooking; the rooftree decays and falls
On the empty lodge, and the winds subvert deserted walls."
Therewithal, to the fuel, he laid the glowing coal;
And the redness ran in the mass and burrowed within like a mole,
And copious smoke was conceived. But, as when a dam is to burst,
The water lips it and crosses in silver trickles at first,
And then, of a sudden, whelms and bears it away forthright;
So now, in a moment, the flame sprang and towered in the night,

And wrestled and roared in the wind, and high over house and tree,
Stood, like a streaming torch, enlightening land and sea.
But the mother of Támatéa threw her arms abroad,
"Pyre of my son," she shouted, "debited vengeance of God,
Late, late, I behold you, yet I behold you at last,
And glory, beholding! For now are the days of my agony past,
The lust that famished my soul now eats and drinks its desire,
And they that encompassed my son shrivel alive in the fire.
Tenfold precious the vengeance that comes after lingering years!
Ye quenched the voice of my singer? — hark, in your dying ears,
The song of the conflagration! Ye left me a widow alone?
— Behold, the whole of your race consumes, sinew and bone
And torturing flesh together: man, mother, and maid
Heaped in a common shambles; and already, borne by the trade,
The smoke of your dissolution darkens the stars of night."
Thus she spoke, and her stature grew in the people's sight.

III

RAHÉRO

Rahéro was there in the hall asleep: beside him his wife,
Comely, a mirthful woman, one that delighted in life;
And a girl that was ripe for marriage, shy and sly as a mouse;
And a boy, a climber of trees: all the hopes of his house.
Unwary, with open hands, he slept in the midst of his folk,
And dreamed that he heard a voice crying without, and awoke,
Leaping blindly afoot like one from a dream that he fears.
A hellish glow and clouds were about him; — it roared in his ears
Like the sound of the cataract fall that plunges sudden and steep;
And Rahéro swayed as he stood, and his reason was still asleep.
Now the flame struck hard on the house, wind-wielded, a fracturing blow,
And the end of the roof was burst and fell on the sleepers below;
And the lofty hall, and the feast, and the prostrate bodies of folk,
Shone red in his eyes a moment, and then were swallowed of smoke.
In the mind of Rahéro clearness came; and he opened his throat;
And as when a squall comes sudden, the straining sail of a boat

Thunders aloud and bursts, so thundered the voice of the man.
— "The wind and the rain!" he shouted, the mustering word of the clan,
And "Up!" and "To arms, men of Vaiau!" But silence replied,
Or only the voice of the gusts of the fire, and nothing beside.
Rahéro stooped and groped. He handled his womankind,
But the fumes of the fire and the kava had quenched the life of their mind,
And they lay like pillars prone; and his hand encountered the boy,
And there sprang in the gloom of his soul a sudden lightning of joy.
"Him can I save!" he thought, "if I were speedy enough."
And he loosened the cloth from his loins, and swaddled the child in the stuff:
And about the strength of his neck he knotted the burden well.
There where the roof had fallen, it roared like the mouth of hell.
Thither Rahéro went, stumbling on senseless folk,
And grappled a post of the house, and began to climb in the smoke:
The last alive of Vaiau; and the son borne by the sire.
The post glowed in the grain with ulcers of eating fire,
And the fire bit to the blood and mangled his hands and thighs;
And the fumes sang in his head like wine and stung in his eyes;
And still he climbed, and came to the top, the place of proof,
And thrust a hand through the flame, and clambered alive on the roof.

But even as he did so, the wind, in a garment of flames and pain,
Wrapped him from head to heel; and the waistcloth parted in twain;
And the living fruit of his loins dropped in the fire below.
About the blazing feast-house clustered the eyes of the foe,
Watching, hand upon weapon, lest ever a soul should flee,
Shading the brow from the glare, straining the neck to see.
Only, to leeward, the flames in the wind swept far and wide,
And the forest sputtered on fire; and there might no man abide.
Thither Rahéro crept, and dropped from the burning eaves,
And crouching low to the ground, in a treble covert of leaves
And fire and volleying smoke, ran for the life of his soul
Unseen; and behind him under a furnace of ardent coal,

Cairned with a wonder of flame, and blotting the night with smoke,
Blazed and were smelted together the bones of all his folk.
He fled unguided at first; but hearing the breakers roar,
Thitherward shaped his way, and came at length to the shore.
Sound-limbed he was: dry-eyed; but smarted in every part;
And the mighty cage of his ribs heaved on his straining heart
With sorrow and rage. And "Fools!" he cried, "fools of Vaiau,
Heads of swine — gluttons — Alas! and where are they now?
Those that I played with, those that nursed me, those that I nursed?
God, and I outliving them! I, the least and the worst —
I, that thought myself crafty, snared by this herd of swine,
In the tortures of hell and desolate, stripped of all that was mine:
All! — my friends and my fathers — the silver heads of yore
That trooped to the council, the children that ran to the open door
Crying with innocent voices and clasping a father's knees!
And mine, my wife — my daughter — my sturdy climber of trees,
Ah, never to climb again!"
Thus in the dusk of the night
(For clouds rolled in the sky and the moon was swallowed from sight),
Pacing and gnawing his fists, Rahéro raged by the shore.
Vengeance: that must be his. But much was to do before;
And first a single life to be snatched from a deadly place,
A life, the root of revenge, surviving plant of the race:
And next the race to be raised anew, and the lands of the clan
Repeopled. So Rahéro designed, a prudent man
Even in wrath, and turned for the means of revenge and escape:
A boat to be seized by stealth, a wife to be taken by rape.
Still was the dark lagoon; beyond on the coral wall,
He saw the breakers shine, he heard them bellow and fall.
Alone, on the top of the reef, a man with a flaming brand
Walked, gazing and pausing, a fish-spear poised in his hand.
The foam boiled to his calf when the mightier breakers came,
And the torch shed in the wind scattering tufts of flame
Afar on the dark lagoon a canoe lay idly at wait:
A figure dimly guiding it: surely the fisherman's mate.
Rahéro saw and he smiled. He straightened his mighty thews:
Naked, with never a weapon, and covered with scorch and bruise,
He straightened his arms, he filled the void of his body with breath,
And, strong as the wind in his manhood, doomed the fisher to death.
Silent he entered the water, and silently swam, and came
There where the fisher walked, holding on high the flame.
Loud on the pier of the reef volleyed the breach of the sea;
And hard at the back of the man, Rahéro crept to his knee
On the coral, and suddenly sprang and seized him, the elder hand
Clutching the joint of his throat, the other snatching the brand
Ere it had time to fall, and holding it steady and high.
Strong was the fisher, brave, and swift of mind and of eye —
Strongly he threw in the clutch; but Rahéro resisted the strain,
And jerked, and the spine of life snapped with a crack in twain,
And the man came slack in his hands and tumbled a lump at his feet.
One moment: and there, on the reef, where the breakers whitened and beat,
Rahéro was standing alone, glowing, and scorched and bare,

A victor unknown of any, raising the torch in the air.
But once he drank of his breath, and instantly set him to fish
Like a man intent upon supper at home and a savoury dish.

For what should the woman have seen? A man with a torch — and then
A moment's blur of the eyes — and a man with a torch again.
And the torch had scarcely been shaken. "Ah, surely," Rahéro said,
"She will deem it a trick of the eyes, a fancy born in the head;
But time must be given the fool to nourish a fool's belief."
So for a while, a sedulous fisher, he walked the reef,
Pausing at times and gazing, striking at times with the spear:
— Lastly, uttered the call; and even as the boat drew near,
Like a man that was done with its use, tossed the torch in the sea.
Lightly he leaped on the boat beside the woman; and she
Lightly addressed him, and yielded the paddle and place to sit;
For now the torch was extinguished the night was black as the pit.
Rahéro set him to row, never a word he spoke,
And the boat sang in the water urged by his vigorous stroke.
— "What ails you?" the woman asked, "and why did you drop the brand?
We have only to kindle another as soon as we come to land."
Never a word Rahéro replied, but urged the canoe.
And a chill fell on the woman. — "Atta! speak! is it you?
Speak! Why are you silent? Why do you bend aside?
Wherefore steer to the seaward?" thus she panted and cried.
Never a word from the oarsman, toiling there in the dark;
But right for a gate of the reef he silently headed the bark,

And wielding the single paddle with passionate sweep on sweep,
Drove her, the little fitted, forth on the open deep.
And fear, there where she sat, froze the woman to stone:
Not fear of the crazy boat and the weltering deep alone;
But a keener fear of the night, the dark, and the ghostly hour,
And the thing that drove the canoe with more than a mortal's power
And more than a mortal's boldness. For much she knew of the dead
That haunt and fish upon reefs, toiling, like men, for bread,
And traffic with human fishers, or slay them and take their ware,
Till the hour when the star of the dead goes down, and the morning air
Blows, and the cocks are singing on shore. And surely she knew
The speechless thing at her side belonged to the grave.
It blew
All night from the south; all night, Rahéro contended and kept
The prow to the cresting sea; and, silent as though she slept,
The woman huddled and quaked. And now was the peep of day.
High and long on their left the mountainous island lay;
And over the peaks of Taiárapu arrows of sunlight struck.
On shore the birds were beginning to sing: the ghostly ruck
Of the buried had long ago returned to the covered grave;
And here on the sea, the woman, waxing suddenly brave,
Turned her swiftly about and looked in the face of the man.
And sure he was none that she knew, none of her country or clan:

A stranger, mother-naked, and marred with the marks of fire,
But comely and great of stature, a man to obey and admire.
And Rahéro regarded her also, fixed, with a frowning face,

Judging the woman's fitness to mother a warlike race.
Broad of shoulder, ample of girdle, long in the thigh,
Deep of bosom she was, and bravely supported his eye.
"Woman," said he, "last night the men of your folk —
Man, woman, and maid, smothered my race in smoke.
It was done like cowards; and I, a mighty man of my hands,
Escaped, a single life; and now to the empty lands
And smokeless hearths of my people, sail, with yourself, alone.
Before your mother was born, the die of to-day was thrown
And you selected: — your husband, vainly striving, to fall
Broken between these hands: — yourself to be severed from all,
The places, the people, you love — home, kindred, and clan —
And to dwell in a desert and bear the babes of a kinless man."

THE FEAST OF FAMINE

MARQUESAN MANNERS

I

THE PRIEST'S VIGIL

    In all the land of the tribe was neither fish nor fruit,
And the deepest pit of popoi stood empty to the foot.
The clans upon the left and the clans upon the right
Now oiled their carven maces and scoured their daggers bright;
They gat them to the thicket, to the deepest of the shade,
And lay with sleepless eyes in the deadly ambuscade.
And oft in the starry even the song of morning rose,
What time the oven smoked in the country of their foes;
For oft to loving hearts, and waiting ears and sight,
The lads that went to forage returned not with the night.
Now first the children sickened, and then the women paled,
And the great arms of the warrior no more for war availed.
Hushed was the deep drum, discarded was the dance;
And those that met the priest now glanced at him askance.
The priest was a man of years, his eyes were ruby-red,
He neither feared the dark nor the terrors of the dead,
He knew the songs of races, the names of ancient date;
And the beard upon his bosom would have bought the chief's estate.
He dwelt in a high-built lodge, hard by the roaring shore,
Raised on a noble terrace and with tikis at the door.
Within it was full of riches, for he served his nation well,
And full of the sound of breakers, like the hollow of a shell.
For weeks he let them perish, gave never a helping sign,
But sat on his oiled platform to commune with the divine,

But sat on his high terrace, with the tikis by his side,
And stared on the blue ocean, like a parrot, ruby-eyed.
Dawn as yellow as sulphur leaped on the mountain height:
Out on the round of the sea the gems of the morning light,
Up from the round of the sea the streamers of the sun; —
But down in the depths of the valley the day was not begun.
In the blue of the woody twilight burned red the cocoa-husk,
And the women and men of the clan went forth to bathe in the dusk,
A word that began to go round, a word, a whisper, a start:
Hope that leaped in the bosom, fear that knocked on the heart:
"See, the priest is not risen — look, for his door is fast!
He is going to name the victims; he is going to help us at last."
Thrice rose the sun to noon; and ever, like one of the dead,
The priest lay still in his house, with the roar of the sea in his head;
There was never a foot on the floor, there was never a whisper of speech;
Only the leering tikis stared on the blinding beach.
Again were the mountains fired, again the morning broke;
And all the houses lay still, but the house of the priest awoke.
Close in their covering roofs lay and trembled the clan,
But the aged, red-eyed priest ran forth like a lunatic man;

And the village panted to see him in the jewels of death again,
In the silver beards of the old and the hair of women slain.

Frenzy shook in his limbs, frenzy shone in his eyes,
And still and again as he ran, the valley rang with his cries.
All day long in the land, by cliff and thicket and den,
He ran his lunatic rounds, and howled for the flesh of men;
All day long he ate not, nor ever drank of the brook;
And all day long in their houses the people listened and shook —
All day long in their houses they listened with bated breath,
And never a soul went forth, for the sight of the priest was death.
Three were the days of his running, as the gods appointed of yore,
Two the nights of his sleeping alone in the place of gore:
The drunken slumber of frenzy twice he drank to the lees,
On the sacred stones of the High-place under the sacred trees;
With a lamp at his ashen head he lay in the place of the feast,
And the sacred leaves of the banyan rustled around the priest.
Last, when the stated even fell upon terrace and tree,
And the shade of the lofty island lay leagues away to sea,
And all the valleys of verdure were heavy with manna and musk,
The wreck of the red-eyed priest came gasping home in the dusk.
He reeled across the village, he staggered along the shore,
And between the leering tikis crept groping through his door.
There went a stir through the lodges, the voice of speech awoke;
Once more from the builded platforms arose the evening smoke.

And those who were mighty in war, and those renowned for an art
Sat in their stated seats and talked of the morrow apart.

II

THE LOVERS

Hark! away in the woods — for the ears of love are sharp —
Stealthily, quietly touched, the note of the one-stringed harp.
In the lighted house of her father, why should Taheia start?
Taheia heavy of hair, Taheia tender of heart,
Taheia the well-descended, a bountiful dealer in love,
Nimble of foot like the deer, and kind of eye like the dove?
Sly and shy as a cat, with never a change of face,
Taheia slips to the door, like one that would breathe a space;
Saunters and pauses, and looks at the stars, and lists to the seas;
Then sudden and swift as a cat, she plunges under the trees.
Swift as a cat she runs, with her garment gathered high,
Leaping, nimble of foot, running, certain of eye;
And ever to guide her way over the smooth and the sharp,
Ever nearer and nearer the note of the one-stringed harp;
Till at length, in a glade of the wood, with a naked mountain above,
The sound of the harp thrown down, and she in the arms of her love.
"Rua," — "Taheia," they cry — "my heart, my soul, and my eyes,"
And clasp and sunder and kiss, with lovely laughter and sighs,

"Rua!" — "Taheia, my love," — "Rua, star of my night,
Clasp me, hold me, and love me, single spring of delight."
And Rua folded her close, he folded her near and long,
The living knit to the living, and sang the lover's song:
Night, night it is, night upon the palms.
Night, night it is, the land-wind has blown.
Starry, starry night, over deep and height;
Love, love in the valley, love all alone.
"Taheia, heavy of hair, a foolish thing have we done,
To bind what gods have sundered unkindly into one.
Why should a lowly lover have touched Taheia's skirt,
Taheia the well-descended, and Rua child of the dirt?"
— "On high with the haka-ikis my father sits in state,
Ten times fifty kinsmen salute him in the gate;
Round all his martial body, and in bands across his face,
The marks of the tattooer proclaim his lofty place.
I too, in the hands of the cunning, in the sacred cabin of palm,
Have shrunk like the mimosa, and bleated like the lamb;
Round half my tender body, that none shall clasp but you,
For a crest and a fair adornment go dainty lines of blue.
Love, love, beloved Rua, love levels all degrees,
And the well-tattooed Taheia clings panting to your knees."
— "Taheia, song of the morning, how long is the longest love?
A cry, a clasp of the hands, a star that falls from above!
Ever at morn in the blue, and at night when all is black,
Ever it skulks and trembles with the hunter, Death, on its track.

Hear me, Taheia, death! For tomorrow the priest shall awake,
And the names be named of the victims to bleed for the nation's sake;
And first of the numbered many that shall be slain ere noon,
Rua the child of the dirt, Rua the kinless loon.

For him shall the drum be beat, for him be raised the song,
For him to the sacred High-place the chanting people throng,
For him the oven smoke as for a speechless beast,
And the sire of my Taheia come greedy to the feast."
"Rua, be silent, spare me. Taheia closes her ears.
Pity my yearning heart, pity my girlish years!
Flee from the cruel hands, flee from the knife and coal,
Lie hid in the deeps of the woods, Rua, sire of my soul!"
"Whither to flee, Taheia, whither in all of the land?
The fires of the bloody kitchen are kindled on every hand;
On every hand in the isle a hungry whetting of teeth,
Eyes in the trees above, arms in the brush beneath.
Patience to lie in wait, cunning to follow the sleuth,
Abroad the foes I have fought, and at home the friends of my youth."
"Love, love, beloved Rua, love has a clearer eye,
Hence from the arms of love you go not forth to die.
There, where the broken mountain drops sheer into the glen,
There shall you find a hold from the boldest hunter of men;
There, in the deep recess, where the sun falls only at noon,
And only once in the night enters the light of the moon,

Nor ever a sound but of birds, or the rain when it falls with a shout;
For death and the fear of death beleaguer the valley about.
Tapu it is, but the gods will surely pardon despair;
Tapu, but what of that? If Rua can only dare.
Tapu and tapu and tapu, I know they are every one right;
But the god of every tapu is not always quick to smite.
Lie secret there, my Rua, in the arms of awful gods,
Sleep in the shade of the trees on the couch of the kindly sods,
Sleep and dream of Taheia, Taheia will wake for you;
And whenever the land-wind blows and the woods are heavy with dew,
Alone through the horror of night, with food for the soul of her love,
Taheia the undissuaded will hurry true as the dove."
"Taheia, the pit of the night crawls with treacherous things,
Spirits of ultimate air and the evil souls of things;
The souls of the dead, the stranglers, that perch in the trees of the wood,
Waiters for all things human, haters of evil and good."
"Rua, behold me, kiss me, look in my eyes and read;
Are these the eyes of a maid that would leave her lover in need?
Brave in the eye of day, my father ruled in the fight;
The child of his loins, Taheia, will play the man in the night."
So it was spoken, and so agreed, and Taheia arose
And smiled in the stars and was gone, swift as the swallow goes;
And Rua stood on the hill, and sighed, and followed her flight,
And there were the lodges below, each with its door alight;

From folk that sat on the terrace and drew out the even long
Sudden crowings of laughter, monotonous drone of song;
The quiet passage of souls over his head in the trees;
And from all around the haven the crumbling thunder of seas.
"Farewell, my home," said Rua. "Farewell, O quiet seat!
Tomorrow in all your valleys the drum of death shall beat."

III

THE FEAST

Dawn as yellow as sulphur leaped on the naked peak,
And all the village was stirring, for now was the priest to speak.
Forth on his terrace he came, and sat with the chief in talk;
His lips were blackened with fever, his cheeks were whiter than chalk;
Fever clutched at his hands, fever nodded his head,
But, quiet and steady and cruel, his eyes shone ruby-red.
In the earliest rays of the sun the chief rose up content;
Braves were summoned, and drummers; messengers came and went;
Braves ran to their lodges; weapons were snatched from the wall;
The commons herded together, and fear was over them all.
Festival dresses they wore, but the tongue was dry in their mouth,
And the blinking eyes in their faces skirted from north to south.

Now to the sacred enclosure gathered the greatest and least,
And from under the shade of the banyan arose the voice of the feast,
The frenzied roll of the drum, and a swift monotonous song.
Higher the sun swam up; the trade-wind level and strong
Awoke in the tops of the palms and rattled the fans aloud,
And over the garlanded heads and shining robes of the crowd
Tossed the spiders of shadow, scattered the jewels of sun.
Forty the tale of the drums, and the forty throbbed like one;
A thousand hearts in the crowd, and the even chorus of song,
Swift as the feet of a runner, trampled a thousand strong.
And the old men leered at the ovens and licked their lips for the food;
And the women stared at the lads, and laughed and looked to the wood.
As when the sweltering baker, at night, when the city is dead,
Alone in the trough of labour treads and fashions the bread;
So in the heat, and the reek, and the touch of woman and man,
The naked spirit of evil kneaded the hearts of the clan.
Now cold was at many a heart, and shaking in many a seat;
For there were the empty baskets, but who was to furnish the meat?
For here was the nation assembled, and there were the ovens anigh,
And out of a thousand singers nine were numbered to die.

Till, of a sudden, a shock, a mace in the air, a yell,
And, struck in the edge of the crowd, the first of the victims fell.
Terror and horrible glee divided the shrinking clan,
Terror of what was to follow, glee for a diet of man.
Frenzy hurried the chant, frenzy rattled the drums;
The nobles, high on the terrace, greedily mouthed their thumbs;
And once and again and again, in the ignorant crowd below,
Once and again and again descended the murderous blow.
Now smoked the oven, and now, with the cutting lip of a shell,
A butcher of ninety winters jointed the bodies well.
Unto the carven lodge, silent, in order due,
The grandees of the nation one after one withdrew;
And a line of laden bearers brought to the terrace foot,
On poles across their shoulders, the last reserve of fruit.
The victims bled for the nobles in the old appointed way;
The fruit was spread for the commons, for all should eat to-day.

And now was the kava brewed, and now the cocoa ran,
Now was the hour of the dance for child and woman and man;
And mirth was in every heart and a garland on every head,
And all was well with the living and well with the eight who were dead.
Only the chiefs and the priest talked and consulted a while:
"Tomorrow," they said, and "Tomorrow," and nodded and seemed to smile:
"Rua the child of dirt, the creature of common clay,
Rua must die tomorrow, since Rua is gone to-day."

Out of the groves of the valley, where clear the blackbirds sang,
Sheer from the trees of the valley the face of the mountain sprang;
Sheer and bare it rose, unscalable barricade,
Beaten and blown against by the generous draught of the trade.
Dawn on its fluted brow painted rainbow light,
Close on its pinnacled crown trembled the stars at night.
Here and there in a cleft clustered contorted trees,
Or the silver beard of a stream hung and swung in the breeze,
High overhead, with a cry, the torrents leaped for the main,
And silently sprinkled below in thin perennial rain.
Dark in the staring noon, dark was Rua's ravine,
Damp and cold was the air, and the face of the cliffs was green.
Here, in the rocky pit, accursed already of old,
On a stone in the midst of a river, Rua sat and was cold.
"Valley of mid-day shadows, valley of silent falls,"
Rua sang, and his voice went hollow about the walls,
"Valley of shadow and rock, a doleful prison to me,
What is the life you can give to a child of the sun and the sea?"
And Rua arose and came to the open mouth of the glen,
Whence he beheld the woods, and the sea, and houses of men.
Wide blew the riotous trade, and smelt in his nostrils good;
It bowed the boats on the bay, and tore and divided the wood;
It smote and sundered the groves as Moses smote with the rod,
And the streamers of all the trees blew like banners abroad;

And ever and on, in a lull, the trade-wind brought him along
A far-off patter of drums and a far-off whisper of song.
Swift as the swallow's wings, the diligent hands on the drum
Fluttered and hurried and throbbed. "Ah, woe that I hear you come,"
Rua cried in his grief, "a sorrowful sound to me,
Mounting far and faint from the resonant shore of the sea!
Woe in the song! for the grave breathes in the singers' breath,
And I hear in the tramp of the drums the beat of the heart of death.
Home of my youth! no more through all the length of the years,
No more to the place of the echoes of early laughter and tears,
No more shall Rua return; no more as the evening ends,
To crowded eyes of welcome, to the reaching hands of friends."
All day long from the High-place the drums and the singing came,
And the even fell, and the sun went down, a wheel of flame;
And night came gleaning the shadows and hushing the sounds of the wood;
And silence slept on all, where Rua sorrowed and stood.
But still from the shore of the bay the sound of the festival rang,
And still the crowd in the High-place danced and shouted and sang.
Now over all the isle terror was breathed abroad
Of shadowy hands from the trees and shadowy snares in the sod;

And before the nostrils of night, the shuddering hunter of men
Hurried, with beard on shoulder, back to his lighted den.
"Taheia, here to my side!" — "Rua, my Rua, you!"
And cold from the clutch of terror, cold with the damp of the dew,
Taheia, heavy of hair, leaped through the dark to his arms;
Taheia leaped to his clasp, and was folded in from alarms.
"Rua, beloved, here, see what your love has brought;
Coming — alas! returning — swift as the shuttle of thought;
Returning, alas! for tonight, with the beaten drum and the voice,
In the shine of many torches must the sleepless clan rejoice;
And Taheia the well-descended, the daughter of chief and priest,
Taheia must sit in her place in the crowded bench of the feast."
So it was spoken; and she, girding her garment high,
Fled and was swallowed of woods, swift as the sight of an eye.
Night over isle and sea rolled her curtain of stars,
Then a trouble awoke in the air, the east was banded with bars;
Dawn as yellow as sulphur leaped on the mountain height;
Dawn, in the deepest glen, fell a wonder of light;
High and clear stood the palms in the eye of the brightening east,
And lo! from the sides of the sea the broken sound of the feast!

As, when in days of summer, through open windows, the fly
Swift as a breeze and loud as a trump goes by,
But when frosts in the field have pinched the wintering mouse,
Blindly noses and buzzes and hums in the firelit house:
So the sound of the feast gallantly trampled at night,
So it staggered and drooped, and droned in the morning light.

IV

THE RAID

It chanced that as Rua sat in the valley of silent falls
He heard a calling of doves from high on the cliffy walls.
Fire had fashioned of yore, and time had broken, the rocks;
There were rooting crannies for trees and nesting-places for flocks;
And he saw on the top of the cliffs, looking up from the pit of the shade,
A flicker of wings and sunshine, and trees that swung in the trade.
"The trees swing in the trade," quoth Rua, doubtful of words,
"And the sun stares from the sky, but what should trouble the birds?"
Up from the shade he gazed, where high the parapet shone,
And he was aware of a ledge and of things that moved thereon.
"What manner of things are these? Are they spirits abroad by day?
Or the foes of my clan that are come, bringing death by a perilous way?"

The valley was gouged like a vessel, and round like the vessel's lip,
With a cape of the side of the hill thrust forth like the bows of a ship.
On the top of the face of the cape a volley of sun struck fair,
And the cape overhung like a chin a gulf of sunless air.
"Silence, heart! What is that? — that, which flickered and shone,
Into the sun for an instant, and in an instant gone?
Was it a warrior's plume, a warrior's girdle of hair?
Swung in the loop of a rope, is he making a bridge of the air?"
Once and again Rua saw, in the trenchant edge of the sky,
The giddy conjuring done. And then, in the blink of an eye,
A scream caught in with the breath, a whirling packet of limbs,
A lump that dived in the gulf, more swift than a dolphin swims;
And there was a lump at his feet, and eyes were alive in the lump.
Sick was the soul of Rua, ambushed close in a clump;
Sick of soul he drew near, making his courage stout;
And he looked in the face of the thing, and the life of the thing went out.
And he gazed on the tattooed limbs, and, behold, he knew the man:
Hoka, a chief of the Vais, the truculent foe of his clan:
Hoka a moment since that stepped in the loop of the rope,
Filled with the lust of war, and alive with courage and hope.
Again to the giddy cornice Rua lifted his eyes,
And again beheld men passing in the armpit of the skies.

"Foes of my race!" cried Rua, "the mouth of Rua is true:
Never a shark in the deep is nobler of soul than you.
There was never a nobler foray, never a bolder plan;
Never a dizzier path was trod by the children of man;
And Rua, your evildoer through all the days of his years,
Counts it honour to hate you, honour to fall by your spears."
And Rua straightened his back. "O Vais, a scheme for a scheme!"
Cried Rua and turned and descended the turbulent stair of the stream,
Leaping from rock to rock as the water-wagtail at home
Flits through resonant valleys and skims by boulder and foam.
And Rua burst from the glen and leaped on the shore of the brook,
And straight for the roofs of the clan his vigorous way he took.
Swift were the heels of his flight, and loud behind as he went
Rattled the leaping stones on the line of his long descent.

And ever he thought as he ran, and caught at his gasping breath,
"O the fool of a Rua, Rua that runs to his death!
But the right is the right," thought Rua, and ran like the wind on the foam,
"The right is the right for ever, and home for ever home.
For what though the oven smoke? And what though I die ere morn?
There was I nourished and tended, and there was Taheia born."
Noon was high on the High-place, the second noon of the feast;
And heat and shameful slumber weighed on people and priest;

And the heart drudged slow in bodies heavy with monstrous meals;
And the senseless limbs were scattered abroad like spokes of wheels;
And crapulous women sat and stared at the stones anigh
With a bestial droop of the lip and a swinish rheum in the eye.
As about the dome of the bees in the time for the drones to fall,
The dead and the maimed are scattered, and lie, and stagger, and crawl;
So on the grades of the terrace, in the ardent eye of the day,
The half-awake and the sleepers clustered and crawled and lay;
And loud as the dome of the bees, in the time of a swarming horde,
A horror of many insects hung in the air and roared.
Rua looked and wondered; he said to himself in his heart:
"Poor are the pleasures of life, and death is the better part."
But lo! on the higher benches a cluster of tranquil folk
Sat by themselves, nor raised their serious eyes, nor spoke:
Women with robes unruffled and garlands duly arranged,
Gazing far from the feast with faces of people estranged;
And quiet amongst the quiet, and fairer than all the fair,
Taheia, the well-descended, Taheia, heavy of hair.
And the soul of Rua awoke, courage enlightened his eyes
And he uttered a summoning shout and called on the clan to rise.
Over against him at once, in the spotted shade of the trees,
Owlish and blinking creatures scrambled to hands and knees;

On the grades of the sacred terrace, the driveller woke to fear,
And the hand of the ham-drooped warrior brandished a wavering spear.
And Rua folded his arms, and scorn discovered his teeth;
Above the war-crowd gibbered, and Rua stood smiling beneath.
Thick, like leaves in the autumn, faint, like April sleet,
Missiles from tremulous hands quivered around his feet;
And Taheia leaped from her place; and the priest, the ruby-eyed,
Ran to the front of the terrace, and brandished his arms and cried:
"Hold, O fools, he brings tidings!" and "Hold, 'tis the love of my heart!"
Till lo! in front of the terrace, Rua pierced with a dart.
Taheia cherished his head, and the aged priest stood by,
And gazed with eyes of ruby at Rua's darkening eye.
"Taheia, here is the end, I die a death for a man.
I have given the life of my soul to save an unsavable clan.
See them, the drooping of hams! behold me the blinking crew;
Fifty spears they cast, and one of fifty true!
And you, O priest, the foreteller, foretell for yourself if you can,
Foretell the hour of the day when the Vais shall burst on your clan!
By the head of the tapu cleft, with death and fire in their hand,
Thick and silent like ants, the warriors swarm in the land."
And they tell that when next the sun had climbed to the noonday skies,
It shone on the smoke of feasting in the country of the Vais.

TICONDEROGA

A LEGEND OF THE WEST HIGHLANDS

TICONDEROGA

    This is the tale of the man
    Who heard a word in the night
    In the land of the heathery hills,
    In the days of the feud and the fight.
    By the sides of the rainy sea,
    Where never a stranger came,
    On the awful lips of the dead,
    He heard the outlandish name.
    It sang in his sleeping ears,
    It hummed in his waking head:
    The name — Ticonderoga,
    The utterance of the dead.

I

THE SAYING OF THE NAME

On the loch-sides of Appin,
When the mist blew from the sea,
A Stewart stood with a Cameron:
An angry man was he.
The blood beat in his ears,
The blood ran hot to his head,
The mist blew from the sea,
And there was the Cameron dead.
"O, what have I done to my friend,
O, what have I done to mysel',
That he should be cold and dead,
And I in the danger of all?

"Nothing but danger about me,
Danger behind and before,
Death at wait in the heather
In Appin and Mamore,
Hate at all of the ferries,
And death at each of the fords,
Camerons priming gun-locks
And Camerons sharpening swords."
But this was a man of counsel,
This was a man of a score,
There dwelt no pawkier Stewart
In Appin or Mamore.
He looked on the blowing mist,
He looked on the awful dead,
And there came a smile on his face
And there slipped a thought in his head.
Out over cairn and moss,
Out over scrog and scaur,
He ran as runs the clansman
That bears the cross of war.
His heart beat in his body,
His hair clove to his face,
When he came at last in the gloaming
To the dead man's brother's place.
The east was white with the moon,
The west with the sun was red,
And there, in the house-doorway,
Stood the brother of the dead.
"I have slain a man to my danger,
I have slain a man to my death.
I put my soul in your hands,"
The panting Stewart saith.

"I lay it bare in your hands,
For I know your hands are leal;
And be you my targe and bulwark
From the bullet and the steel."

Then up and spoke the Cameron,
And gave him his hand again:
"There shall never a man in Scotland
Set faith in me in vain;
And whatever man you have slaughtered,
Of whatever name or line,
By my sword and yonder mountain,
I make your quarrel mine.
I bid you in to my fireside,
I share with you house and hall;
It stands upon my honour
To see you safe from all."
It fell in the time of midnight,
When the fox barked in the den,
And the plaids were over the faces
In all the houses of men,
That as the living Cameron
Lay sleepless on his bed,
Out of the night and the other world,
Came in to him the dead.
"My blood is on the heather,
My bones are on the hill;
There is joy in the home of ravens
That the young shall eat their fill.
My blood is poured in the dust,
My soul is spilled in the air;
And the man that has undone me
Sleeps in my brother's care."

"I'm wae for your death, my brother,
But if all of my house were dead,
I couldna withdraw the plighted hand,
Nor break the word once said."
"O, what shall I say to our father,
In the place to which I fare?
O, what shall I say to our mother,
Who greets to see me there?
And to all the kindly Camerons
That have lived and died long-syne —
Is this the word you send them,
Fause-hearted brother mine?"
"It's neither fear nor duty,
It's neither quick nor dead,
Shall gar me withdraw the plighted hand,
Or break the word once said."
Thrice in the time of midnight,
When the fox barked in the den,
And the plaids were over the faces
In all the houses of men,
Thrice as the living Cameron
Lay sleepless on his bed,
Out of the night and the other world
Came in to him the dead,

And cried to him for vengeance
On the man that laid him low;
And thrice the living Cameron
Told the dead Cameron, no.
"Thrice have you seen me, brother,
But now shall see me no more,
Till you meet your angry fathers
Upon the farther shore.

Thrice have I spoken, and now,
Before the cock be heard,
I take my leave for ever
With the naming of a word.
It shall sing in your sleeping ears,
It shall hum in your waking head,
The name — Ticonderoga,
And the warning of the dead."
Now when the night was over
And the time of people's fears,
The Cameron walked abroad,
And the word was in his ears.
"Many a name I know,
But never a name like this;
O, where shall I find a skilly man
Shall tell me what it is?"
With many a man he counselled
Of high and low degree,
With the herdsman on the mountains
And the fishers of the sea.
And he came and went unweary,
And read the books of yore,
And the runes that were written of old
On stones upon the moor.
And many a name he was told,
But never the name of his fears —
Never, in east or west,
The name that rang in his ears:
Names of men and of clans;
Names for the grass and the tree,
For the smallest tarn in the mountains,
The smallest reef in the sea:
Names for the high and low,
The names of the craig and the flat;
But in all the land of Scotland,
Never a name like that.

II

THE SEEKING OF THE NAME

And now there was speech in the south,
And a man of the south that was wise,
A periwig'd lord of London,
Called on the clans to rise.
And the riders rode, and the summons
Came to the western shore,
To the land of the sea and the heather,
To Appin and Mamore.
It called on all to gather
From every scrog and scaur,
That loved their fathers' tartan
And the ancient game of war.
And down the watery valley
And up the windy hill,
Once more, as in the olden,
The pipes were sounding shrill;
Again in Highland sunshine
The naked steel was bright;
And the lads, once more in tartan,
Went forth again to fight.
"O, why should I dwell here
With a weird upon my life,
When the clansmen shout for battle
And the war-swords clash in strife?
I canna joy at feast,
I canna sleep in bed,
For the wonder of the word
And the warning of the dead.
It sings in my sleeping ears,
It hums in my waking head,
The name — Ticonderoga,
The utterance of the dead.
Then up, and with the fighting men
To march away from here,
Till the cry of the great war-pipe
Shall drown it in my ear!"
Where flew King George's ensign
The plaided soldiers went:
They drew the sword in Germany,
In Flanders pitched the tent.
The bells of foreign cities
Rang far across the plain:
They passed the happy Rhine,
They drank the rapid Main.
Through Asiatic jungles
The Tartans filed their way,
And the neighing of the war-pipes
Struck terror in Cathay.

"Many a name have I heard," he thought,
"In all the tongues of men,
Full many a name both here and there,
Full many both now and then.
When I was at home in my father's house,
In the land of the naked knee,
Between the eagles that fly in the lift
And the herrings that swim in the sea,
And now that I am a captain-man
With a braw cockade in my hat —
Many a name have I heard," he thought,
"But never a name like that."

III

THE PLACE OF THE NAME

There fell a war in a woody place,
Lay far across the sea,
A war of the march in the mirk midnight
And the shot from behind the tree,
The shaven head and the painted face,
The silent foot in the wood,
In the land of a strange, outlandish tongue
That was hard to be understood.
It fell about the gloaming,
The general stood with his staff,
He stood and he looked east and west
With little mind to laugh.
"Far have I been, and much have I seen,
And kennt both gain and loss,
But here we have woods on every hand
And a kittle water to cross.
Far have I been, and much have I seen,
But never the beat of this;
And there's one must go down to that waterside
To see how deep it is."
It fell in the dusk of the night
When unco things betide,
The skilly captain, the Cameron,
Went down to that waterside.
Canny and soft the captain went;
And a man of the woody land,
With the shaven head and the painted face,
Went down at his right hand.
It fell in the quiet night,
There was never a sound to ken;
But all of the woods to the right and the left
Lay filled with the painted men.

"Far have I been, and much have I seen,
Both as a man and boy,
But never have I set forth a foot,
On so perilous an employ."
It fell in the dusk of the night
When unco things betide,
That he was aware of a captain-man
Drew near to the waterside.
He was aware of his coming
Down in the gloaming alone;
And he looked in the face of the man,
And lo! the face was his own.
"This is my weird," he said,
"And now I ken the worst;
For many shall fall the morn,
But I shall fall with the first.

O, you of the outland tongue,
You of the painted face,
This is the place of my death;
Can you tell me the name of the place?"
"Since the Frenchmen have been here
They have called it Sault-Marie;
But that is a name for priests,
And not for you and me.
It went by another word,"
Quoth he of the shaven head:
"It was called Ticonderoga
In the days of the great dead."
And it fell on the morrow's morning,
In the fiercest of the fight,
That the Cameron bit the dust
As he foretold at night;
And far from the hills of heather,
Far from the isles of the sea,
He sleeps in the place of the name
As it was doomed to be.

HEATHER ALE

A GALLOWAY LEGEND

From the bonny bells of heather
They brewed a drink long-syne,
Was sweeter far than honey,
Was stronger far than wine.
They brewed it and they drank it,
And lay in a blessed swound
For days and days together
In their dwellings underground.
There rose a king in Scotland,
A fell man to his foes,
He smote the Picts in battle,
He hunted them like roes.
Over miles of the red mountain
He hunted as they fled,
And strewed the dwarfish bodies
Of the dying and the dead.
Summer came in the country,
Red was the heather bell;
But the manner of the brewing
Was none alive to tell.
In the graves that were like children's
On many a mountain head,
The Brewsters of the Heather
Lay numbered with the dead.
The king in the red moorland
Rode on a summer's day;
And the bees hummed, and the curlews
Cried beside the way.

The king rode, and was angry,
Black was his brow and pale,
To rule in a land of heather
And lack the Heather Ale.
It fortuned that his vassals,
Riding free on the heath,
Came on a stone that was fallen
And vermin hid beneath.
Rudely plucked from their hiding,
Never a word they spoke:
A son and his aged father —
Last of the dwarfish folk.
The king sat high on his charger,
He looked on the little men;
And the dwarfish and swarthy couple
Looked at the king again.
Down by the shore he had them;
And there on the giddy brink —
"I will give you life, ye vermin,
For the secret of the drink."

There stood the son and father;
And they looked high and low;
The heather was red around them,
The sea rumbled below.
And up and spoke the father,
Shrill was his voice to hear:
"I have a word in private,
A word for the royal ear.
"Life is dear to the aged,
And honour a little thing;
I would gladly sell the secret,"
Quoth the Pict to the king.

His voice was small as a sparrow's,
And shrill and wonderful clear;
"I would gladly sell my secret,
Only my son I fear.
"For life is a little matter,
And death is nought to the young;
And I dare not sell my honour
Under the eye of my son.
Take *him*, O king, and bind him,
And cast him far in the deep:
And it's I will tell the secret,
That I have sworn to keep."
They took the son and bound him,
Neck and heels in a thong,
And a lad took him and swung him,
And flung him far and strong,
And the sea swallowed his body,
Like that of a child of ten; —
And there on the cliff stood the father,
Last of the dwarfish men.
"True was the word I told you:
Only my son I feared;
For I doubt the sapling courage
That goes without the beard.
But now in vain is the torture,
Fire shall never avail;
Here dies in my bosom
The secret of Heather Ale."

CHRISTMAS AT SEA

The sheets were frozen hard, and they cut the naked hand;
The decks were like a slide, where a seaman scarce could stand;
The wind was a nor'-wester, blowing squally off the sea;
And cliffs and spouting breakers were the only things a-lee.
They heard the surf a-roaring before the break of day;
But 'twas only with the peep of light we saw how ill we lay.
We tumbled every hand on deck instanter, with a shout,
And we gave her the maintops'l, and stood by to go about.
All day we tacked and tacked between the South Head and the North;
All day we hauled the frozen sheets, and got no further forth;
All day as cold as charity, in bitter pain and dread,
For very life and nature we tacked from head to head.
We gave the South a wider berth, for there the tide-race roared;
But every tack we made we brought the North Head close aboard:
So's we saw the cliffs and houses, and the breakers running high,
And the coastguard in his garden, with his glass against his eye.

The frost was on the village roofs as white as ocean foam;
The good red fires were burning bright in every 'longshore home;
The windows sparkled clear, and the chimneys volleyed out;
And I vow we sniffed the victuals as the vessel went about.
The bells upon the church were rung with a mighty jovial cheer;
For it's just that I should tell you how (of all days in the year)
This day of our adversity was blessèd Christmas morn,
And the house above the coastguard's was the house where I was born.
O well I saw the pleasant room, the pleasant faces there,
My mother's silver spectacles, my father's silver hair;
And well I saw the firelight, like a flight of homely elves,
Go dancing round the china-plates that stand upon the shelves.
And well I knew the talk they had, the talk that was of me,
Of the shadow on the household and the son that went to sea;
And O the wicked fool I seemed, in every kind of way,
To be here and hauling frozen ropes on blessèd Christmas Day.
They lit the high sea-light, and the dark began to fall.
"All hands to loose topgallant sails," I heard the captain call.
"By the Lord, she'll never stand it," our first mate, Jackson, cried.
..."It's the one way or the other, Mr. Jackson," he replied.

She staggered to her bearings, but the sails were new and good,
And the ship smelt up to windward just as though she understood,
As the winter's day was ending, in the entry of the night,
We cleared the weary headland, and passed below the light.
And they heaved a mighty breath, every soul on board but me,
As they saw her nose again pointing handsome out to sea;
But all that I could think of, in the darkness and the cold,
Was just that I was leaving home and my folks were growing old.

A CHILD'S GARDEN OF VERSES

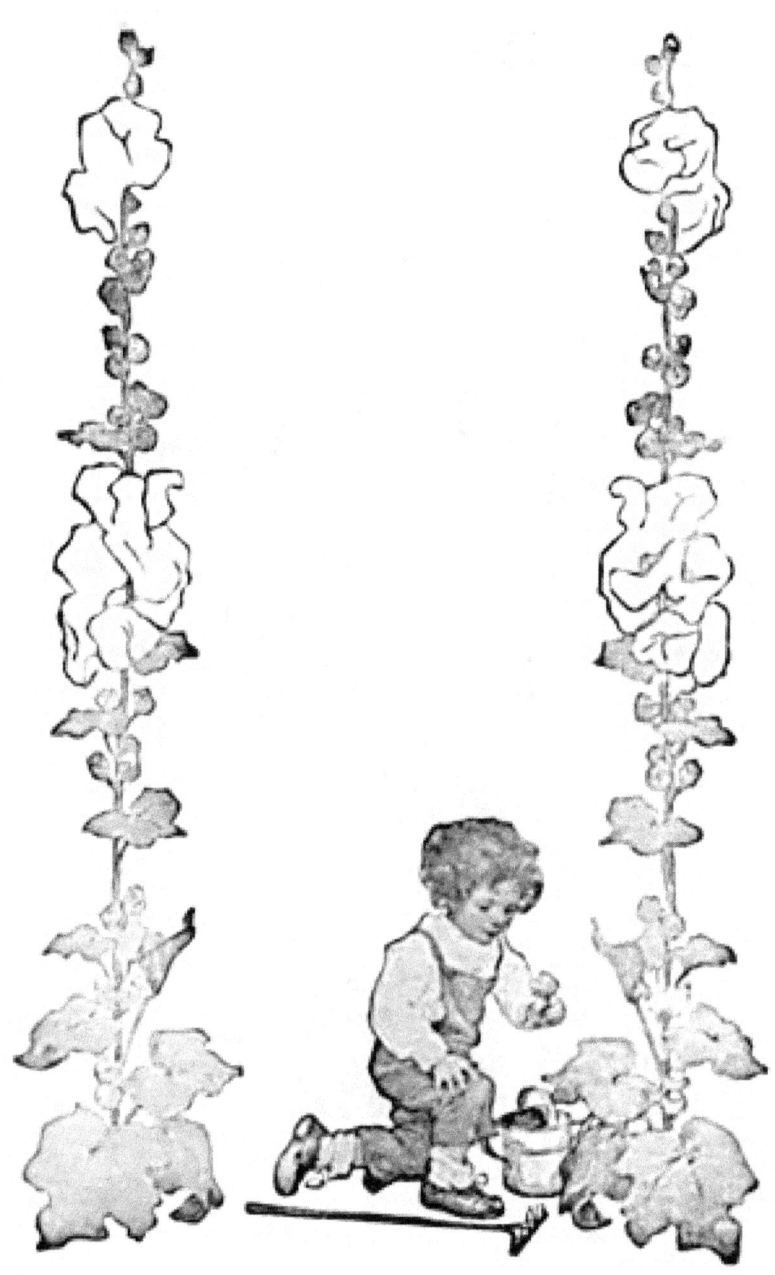

TO ALISON CUNNINGHAM

FROM HER BOY

For the long nights you lay awake
And watched for my unworthy sake:
For your most comfortable hand
That led me through the uneven land:
For all the storybooks you read:

For all the pains you comforted:
For all you pitied, all you bore,
In sad and happy days of yore: —
My second Mother, my first Wife,
The angel of my infant life —
From the sick child, now well and old,
Take, nurse, the little book you hold!

And grant it, Heaven, that all who read
May find as dear a nurse at need,
And every child who lists my rhyme,
In the bright, fireside, nursery clime,
May hear it in as kind a voice
As made my childish days rejoice!
R. L. S.

BED IN SUMMER

In winter I get up at night
And dress by yellow candlelight.
In summer, quite the other way,
I have to go to bed by day.
I have to go to bed and see
The birds still hopping on the tree,
Or hear the grown-up people's feet
Still going past me in the street.
And does it not seem hard to you,
When all the sky is clear and blue,
And I should like so much to play,

To have to go to bed by day?

BED IN SUMMER

Mary

Hans

A THOUGHT

It is very nice to think
The world is full of meat and drink,
With little children saying grace
In every Christian kind of place.

Biddy

Fifine

AT THE SEA-SIDE

When I was down beside the sea
A wooden spade they gave to me
To dig the sandy shore.
My holes were empty like a cup.
In every hole the sea came up,
Till it could come no more.

YOUNG NIGHT-THOUGHT

All night long and every night,
When my mama puts out the light,
I see the people marching by,
As plain as day, before my eye.
Armies and emperors and kings,
All carrying different kinds of things,
And marching in so grand a way,
You never saw the like by day.
So fine a show was never seen
At the great circus on the green;
For every kind of beast and man
Is marching in that caravan.
At first they move a little slow,
But still the faster on they go,
And still beside them close I keep
Until we reach the town of Sleep.

WHOLE DUTY OF CHILDREN

A child should always say what's true
And speak when he is spoken to,
And behave mannerly at table;
At least as far as he is able.

RAIN

The rain is raining all around,
It falls on field and tree,
It rains on the umbrellas here,
And on the ships at sea.

PIRATE STORY

Three of us afloat in the meadow by the swing,
Three of us aboard in the basket on the lea.
Winds are in the air, they are blowing in the spring,
And waves are on the meadow like the waves there are at sea.
Where shall we adventure, to-day that we're afloat,
Wary of the weather and steering by a star?
Shall it be to Africa, a-steering of the boat,
To Providence, or Babylon, or off to Malabar?
Hi! but here's a squadron a-rowing on the sea —
Cattle on the meadow a-charging with a roar!
Quick, and we'll escape them, they're as mad as they can be,
The wicket is the harbour and the garden is the shore.

FOREIGN LANDS

Up into the cherry tree
Who should climb but little me?
I held the trunk with both my hands
And looked abroad on foreign lands.
I saw the next door garden lie,
Adorned with flowers, before my eye,
And many pleasant places more
That I had never seen before.
I saw the dimpling river pass
And be the sky's blue looking-glass;
The dusty roads go up and down
With people tramping in to town.
If I could find a higher tree
Farther and farther I should see,
To where the grown-up river slips
Into the sea among the ships,
To where the roads on either hand
Lead onward into fairy land,
Where all the children dine at five,

And all the playthings come alive.

FOREIGN LANDS

WINDY NIGHTS

Whenever the moon and stars are set,
Whenever the wind is high,
All night long in the dark and wet,
A man goes riding by.
Late in the night when the fires are out,
Why does he gallop and gallop about?
Whenever the trees are crying aloud,
And ships are tossed at sea,
By, on the highway, low and loud,
By at the gallop goes he.
By at the gallop he goes, and then
By he comes back at the gallop again.

TRAVEL

I should like to rise and go
Where the golden apples grow; —
Where below another sky
Parrot islands anchored lie,
And, watched by cockatoos and goats,
Lonely Crusoes building boats; —
Where in sunshine reaching out
Eastern cities, miles about,
Are with mosque and minaret
Among sandy gardens set,
And the rich goods from near and far
Hang for sale in the bazaar; —
Where the Great Wall round China goes,
And on one side the desert blows,
And with bell and voice and drum,
Cities on the other hum; —
Where are forests, hot as fire,
Wide as England, tall as a spire,
Full of apes and cocoanuts
And the negro hunters' huts; —
Where the knotty crocodile
Lies and blinks in the Nile,
And the red flamingo flies
Hunting fish before his eyes; —
Where in jungles, near and far,
Man-devouring tigers are,
Lying close and giving ear
Lest the hunt be drawing near,

Or a comer-by be seen
Swinging in a palanquin; —
Where among the desert sands
Some deserted city stands,
All its children, sweep and prince,
Grown to manhood ages since,
Not a foot in street or house,
Not a stir of child or mouse,

And when kindly falls the night,
In all the town no spark of light.
There I'll come when I'm a man
With a camel caravan;
Light a fire in the gloom
Of some dusty dining-room;
See the pictures on the walls,
Heroes, fights, and festivals;
And in a corner find the toys
Of the old Egyptian boys.

SINGING

Of speckled eggs the birdie sings
And nests among the trees;
The sailor sings of ropes and things
In ships upon the seas.
The children sing in far Japan,
The children sing in Spain;
The organ with the organ man
Is singing in the rain.

LOOKING FORWARD

When I am grown to man's estate
I shall be very proud and great,
And tell the other girls and boys
Not to meddle with my toys.

A GOOD PLAY

We built a ship upon the stairs
All made of the back-bedroom chairs,
And filled it full of sofa pillows
To go a-sailing on the billows.
We took a saw and several nails,
And water in the nursery pails;
And Tom said, "Let us also take
An apple and a slice of cake;" —
Which was enough for Tom and me
To go a-sailing on, till tea.
We sailed along for days and days
And had the very best of plays;
But Tom fell out and hurt his knee,
So there was no one left but me.

WHERE GO THE BOATS?

Dark brown is the river,
Golden is the sand.
It flows along for ever,
With trees on either hand.
Green leaves afloating,

Castles of the foam,
Boats of mine a-boating —
Where will all come home?
On goes the river
And out past the mill,
Away down the valley,
Away down the hill.
Away down the river,
A hundred miles or more,
Other little children
Shall bring my boats ashore.

AUNTIE'S SKIRTS

Whenever Auntie moves around,
Her dresses make a curious sound,
They trail behind her up the floor,
And trundle after through the door.

THE LAND OF COUNTERPANE

When I was sick and lay a-bed,
I had two pillows at my head,
And all my toys beside me lay
To keep me happy all the day.
And sometimes for an hour or so
I watched my leaden soldiers go,
With different uniforms and drills,
Among the bedclothes, through the hills;
And sometimes sent my ships in fleets
All up and down among the sheets;
Or brought my trees and houses out,
And planted cities all about.
I was the giant great and still
That sits upon the pillow-hill,
And sees before him, dale and plain,

The pleasant land of counterpane.

THE LAND OF COUNTERPANE

THE LAND OF NOD

From breakfast on through all the day
At home among my friends I stay,
But every night I go abroad
Afar into the land of Nod.
All by myself I have to go,
With none to tell me what to do —
All alone beside the streams
And up the mountainsides of dreams.

The strangest things are there for me,
Both things to eat and things to see,

And many frightening sights abroad
Till morning in the land of Nod.
Try as I like to find the way,
I never can get back by day,
Nor can remember plain and clear
The curious music that I hear.

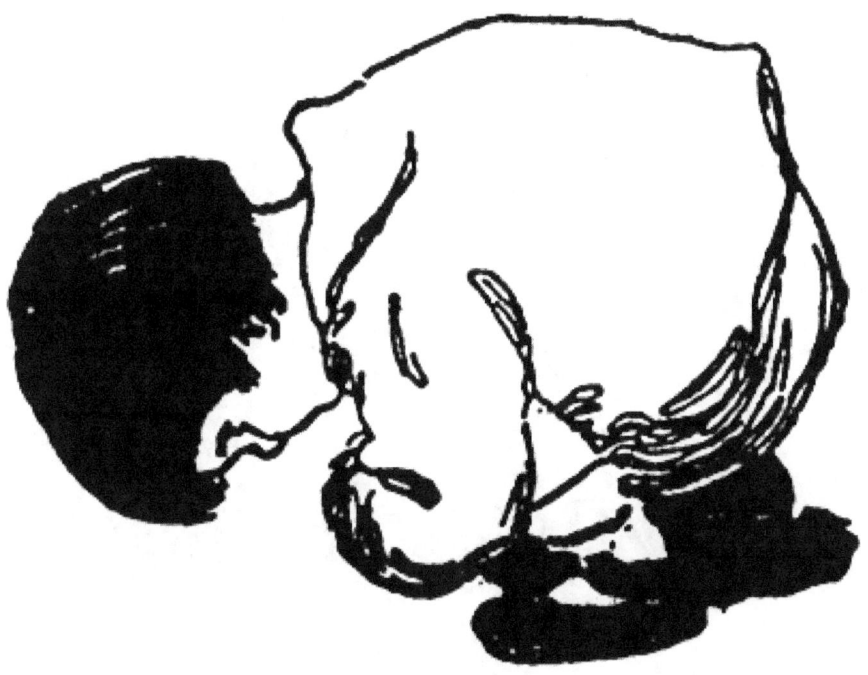

MY SHADOW

I have a little shadow that goes in and out with me,
And what can be the use of him is more than I can see.
He is very, very like me from the heels up to the head;
And I see him jump before me, when I jump into my bed.
The funniest thing about him is the way he likes to grow —
Not at all like proper children, which is always very slow;
For he sometimes shoots up taller like an indiarubber ball,
And he sometimes gets so little that there's none of him at all.
He hasn't got a notion of how children ought to play,
And can only make a fool of me in every sort of way.
He stays so close beside me, he's a coward you can see;
I'd think shame to stick to nursie as that shadow sticks to me!

MY SHADOW

One morning, very early, before the sun was up,
I rose and found the shining dew on every buttercup;

But my lazy little shadow, like an arrant sleepy-head,
Had stayed at home behind me and was fast asleep in bed.

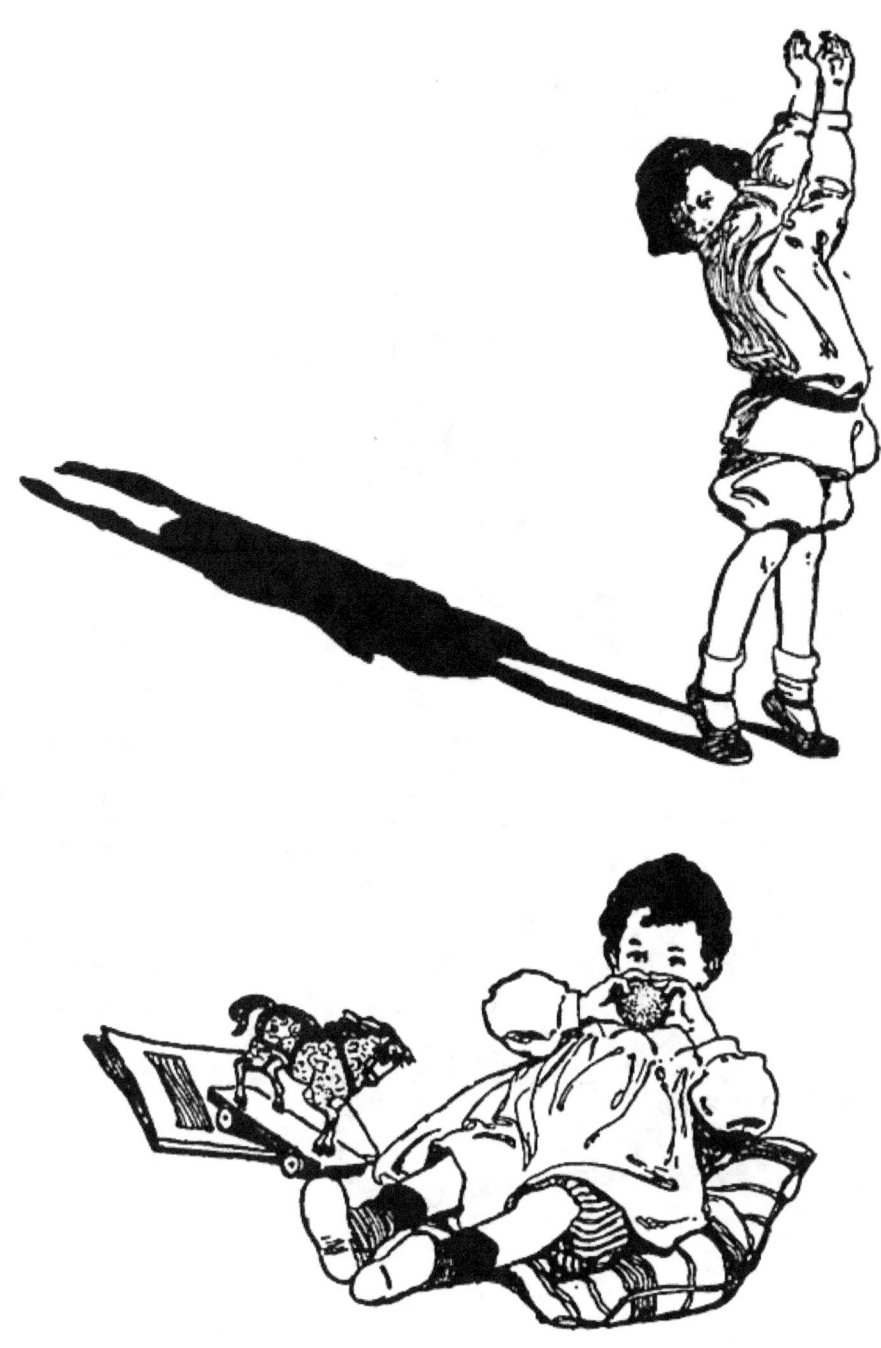

SYSTEM

Every night my prayers I say,
And get my dinner every day;
And every day that I've been good,
I get an orange after food.
The child that is not clean and neat,
With lots of toys and things to eat,
He is a naughty child, I'm sure —
Or else his dear papa is poor.

A GOOD BOY

I woke before the morning, I was happy all the day,
I never said an ugly word, but smiled and stuck to play.
And now at last the sun is going down behind the wood,
And I am very happy, for I know that I've been good.
My bed is waiting cool and fresh, with linen smooth and fair
And I must be off to sleepsin-by, and not forget my prayer.
I know that, till tomorrow I shall see the sun arise,
No ugly dream shall fright my mind, no ugly sight my eyes.
But slumber hold me tightly till I waken in the dawn,
And hear the thrushes singing in the lilacs round the lawn.

ESCAPE AT BEDTIME

The lights from the parlour and kitchen shone out
Through the blinds and the windows and bars;
And high overhead and all moving about,
There were thousands of millions of stars.
There ne'er were such thousands of leaves on a tree,
Nor of people in church or the Park,
As the crowds of the stars that looked down upon me,
And that glittered and winked in the dark.
The Dog, and the Plough, and the Hunter, and all,
And the star of the sailor, and Mars,
These shone in the sky, and the pail by the wall
Would be half full of water and stars.
They saw me at last, and they chased me with cries,
And they soon had me packed into bed;
But the glory kept shining and bright in my eyes,
And the stars going round in my head.

MARCHING SONG

    Bring the comb and play upon it!
    Marching, here we come!
    Willie cocks his highland bonnet,
    Johnnie beats the drum.
    Mary Jane commands the party,
    Peter leads the rear;
    Feet in time, alert and hearty,
    Each a Grenadier!
    All in the most martial manner
    Marching double-quick;
    While the napkin, like a banner,
    Waves upon the stick!
    Here's enough of fame and pillage,
    Great commander Jane!
    Now that we've been round the village,
    Let's go home again.

THE COW

The friendly cow all red and white,
I love with all my heart:
She gives me cream with all her might,
To eat with apple-tart.
She wanders lowing here and there,
And yet she cannot stray,
All in the pleasant open air,
The pleasant light of day;
And blown by all the winds that pass
And wet with all the showers,
She walks among the meadow grass
And eats the meadow flowers.

HAPPY THOUGHT

The world is so full of a number of things,
I'm sure we should all be as happy as kings.

THE WIND

I saw you toss the kites on high
And blow the birds about the sky;
And all around I heard you pass,
Like ladies' skirts across the grass —
O wind, a-blowing all day long,
O wind, that sings so loud a song!
I saw the different things you did,
But always you yourself you hid.
I felt you push, I heard you call,
I could not see yourself at all —
O wind, a-blowing all day long,
O wind, that sings so loud a song!
O you that are so strong and cold,
O blower, are you young or old?
Are you a beast of field and tree,
Or just a stronger child than me?
O wind, a-blowing all day long,
O wind, that sings so loud a song!

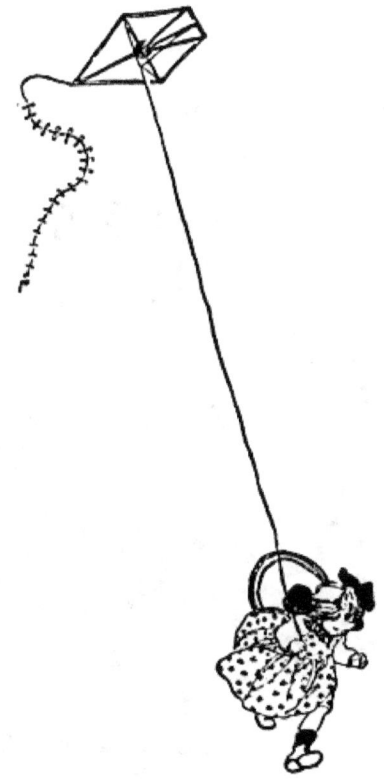

KEEPSAKE MILL

Over the borders, a sin without pardon,
Breaking the branches and crawling below,
Out through the breach in the wall of the garden,
Down by the banks of the river, we go.
Here is the mill with the humming of thunder,
Here is the weir with the wonder of foam,
Here is the sluice with the race running under —
Marvellous places, though handy to home!
Sounds of the village grow stiller and stiller,
Stiller the note of the birds on the hill;
Dusty and dim are the eyes of the miller,
Deaf are his ears with the moil of the mill.
Years may go by, and the wheel in the river
Wheel as it wheels for us, children, to-day,
Wheel and keep roaring and foaming for ever
Long after all of the boys are away.
Home from the Indies and home from the ocean,
Heroes and soldiers we all shall come home;
Still we shall find the old mill wheel in motion,
Turning and churning that river to foam.

You with the bean that I gave when we quarrelled,
I with your marble of Saturday last,
Honoured and old and all gaily apparelled,
Here we shall meet and remember the past.

GOOD AND BAD CHILDREN

Children, you are very little,
And your bones are very brittle;
If you would grow great and stately,
You must try to walk sedately.
You must still be bright and quiet,
And content with simple diet;
And remain, through all bewild'ring,
Innocent and honest children.
Happy hearts and happy faces,
Happy play in grassy places —
That was how, in ancient ages,
Children grew to kings and sages.

But the unkind and the unruly,
And the sort who eat unduly,
They must never hope for glory —
Theirs is quite a different story!
Cruel children, crying babies,
All grew up as geese and gabies,
Hated, as their age increases,
By their nephews and their nieces.

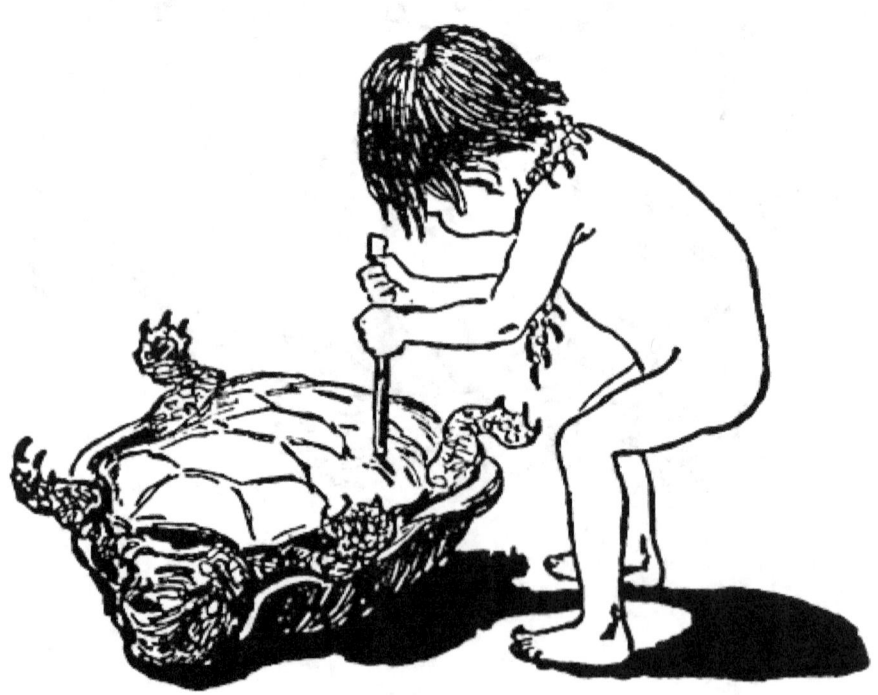

FOREIGN CHILDREN

Little Indian, Sioux or Crow,
Little frosty Eskimo,
Little Turk or Japanee,
Oh! don't you wish that you were me?
You have seen the scarlet trees
And the lions over seas;
You have eaten ostrich eggs,
And turned the turtles off their legs.
Such a life is very fine,
But it's not so nice as mine:
You must often, as you trod,
Have wearied *not* to be abroad.
You have curious things to eat,
I am fed on proper meat;
You must dwell beyond the foam,
But I am safe and live at home.
Little Indian, Sioux or Crow,
Little frosty Eskimo,
Little Turk or Japanee,

Oh! don't you wish that you were me?

FOREIGN CHILDREN

THE SUN TRAVELS

The sun is not a-bed, when I
At night upon my pillow lie;
Still round the earth his way he takes,
And morning after morning makes.
While here at home, in shining day,
We round the sunny garden play,
Each little Indian sleepy-head
Is being kissed and put to bed.
And when at eve I rise from tea,
Day dawns beyond the Atlantic Sea;
And all the children in the West
Are getting up and being dressed.

THE LAMPLIGHTER

My tea is nearly ready and the sun has left the sky.
It's time to take the window to see Leerie going by;
For every night at teatime and before you take your seat,
With lantern and with ladder he comes posting up the street.

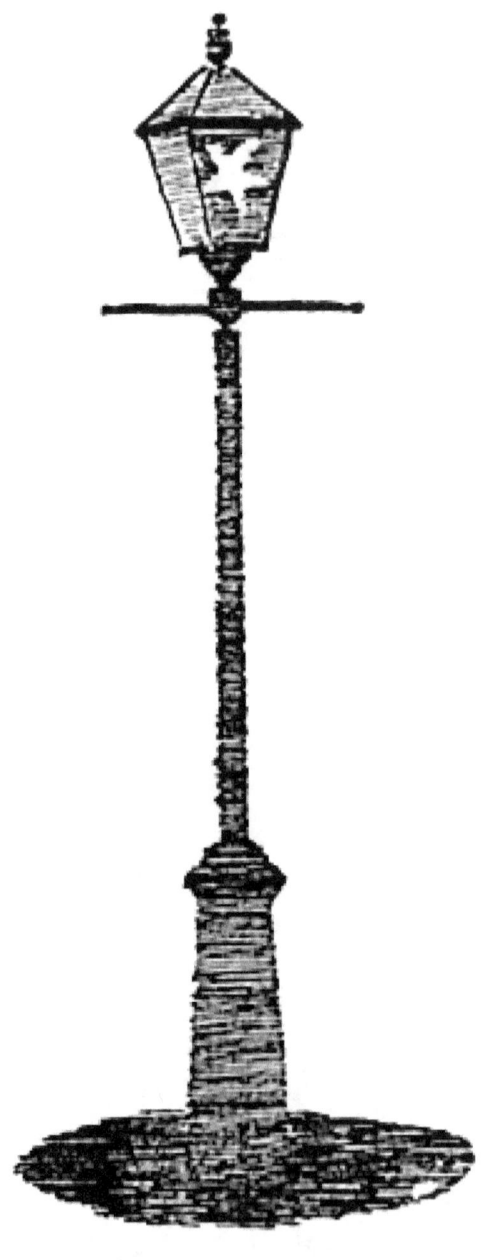

Now Tom would be a driver and Maria go to sea,
And my papa's a banker and as rich as he can be;

But I, when I am stronger and can choose what I'm to do,
O Leerie, I'll go round at night and light the lamps with you!
For we are very lucky, with a lamp before the door,
And Leerie stops to light it as he lights so many more;
And oh! before you hurry by with ladder and with light;
O Leerie, see a little child and nod to him tonight!

MY BED IS A BOAT

My bed is like a little boat;
Nurse helps me in when I embark;
She girds me in my sailor's coat
And starts me in the dark.
At night, I go on board and say
Goodnight to all my friends on shore;
I shut my eyes and sail away
And see and hear no more.
And sometimes things to bed I take,
As prudent sailors have to do;
Perhaps a slice of wedding-cake,
Perhaps a toy or two.

All night across the dark we steer;
But when the day returns at last,
Safe in my room, beside the pier,
I find my vessel fast.

THE MOON

The moon has a face like the clock in the hall;
She shines on thieves on the garden wall,
On streets and field and harbour quays,
And birdies asleep in the forks of the trees.
The squalling cat and the squeaking mouse,
The howling dog by the door of the house,
The bat that lies in bed at noon,
All love to be out by the light of the moon.
But all of the things that belong to the day
Cuddle to sleep to be out of her way;
And flowers and children close their eyes
Till up in the morning the sun shall arise.

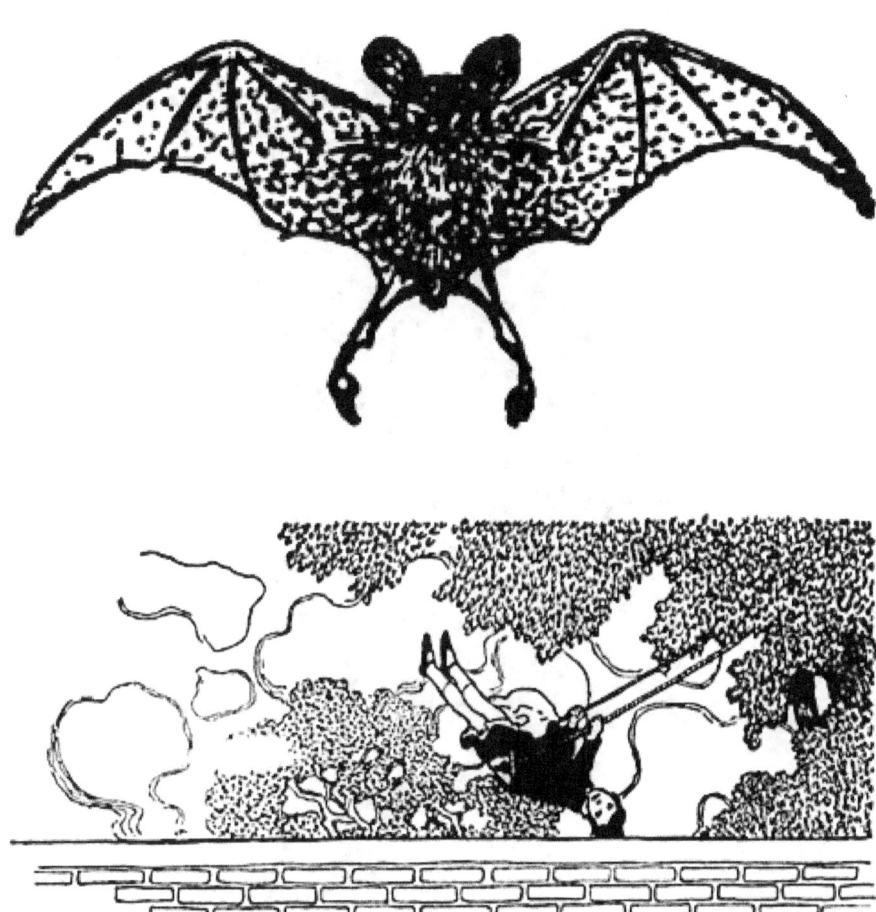

THE SWING

How do you like to go up in a swing,
Up in the air so blue?
Oh, I do think it the pleasantest thing
Ever a child can do!
Up in the air and over the wall,
Till I can see so wide,
Rivers and trees and cattle and all
Over the countryside —
Till I look down on the garden green,
Down on the roof so brown —
Up in the air I go flying again,
Up in the air and down!

TIME TO RISE

A birdie with a yellow bill
Hopped upon the window sill,
Cocked his shining eye and said:
"Ain't you 'shamed, you sleepy-head!"

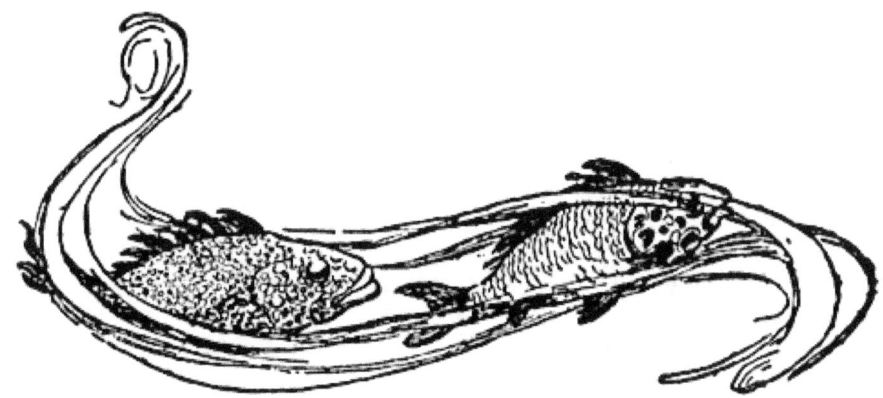

LOOKING-GLASS RIVER

Smooth it glides upon its travel,
Here a wimple, there a gleam —
O the clean gravel!
O the smooth stream!
Sailing blossoms, silver fishes,
Paven pools as clear as air —
How a child wishes
To live down there!
We can see our coloured faces
Floating on the shaken pool
Down in cool places,
Dim and very cool;
Till a wind or water wrinkle,
Dipping marten, plumping trout,
Spreads in a twinkle
And blots all out.

See the rings pursue each other;
All below grows black as night,
Just as if mother
Had blown out the light!
Patience, children, just a minute —
See the spreading circles die;
The stream and all in it
Will clear by-and-by.

FAIRY BREAD

Come up here, O dusty feet!
Here is fairy bread to eat.
Here in my retiring room,
Children, you may dine
On the golden smell of broom
And the shade of pine;
And when you have eaten well,
Fairy stories hear and tell.

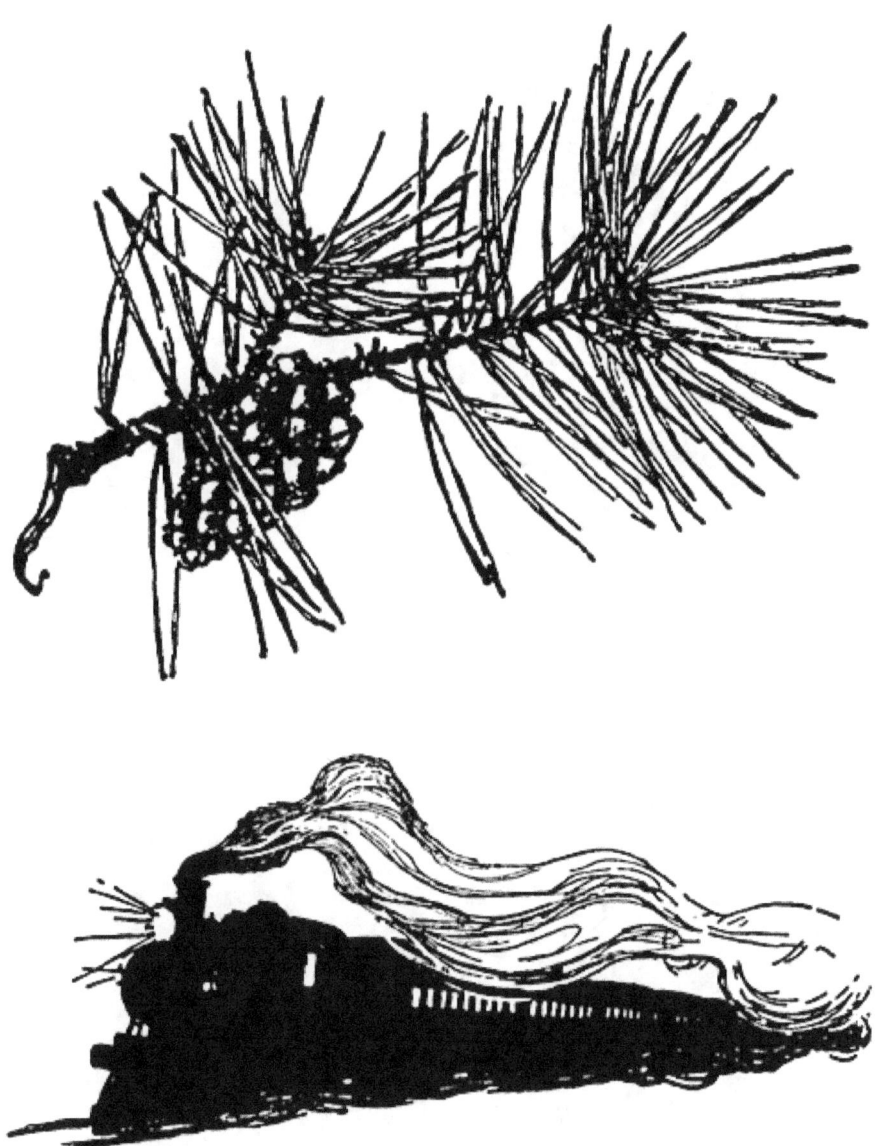

FROM A RAILWAY CARRIAGE

Faster than fairies, faster than witches,
Bridges and houses, hedges and ditches;
And charging along like troops in a battle
All through the meadows the horses and cattle:
All of the sights of the hill and the plain
Fly as thick as driving rain;
And ever again, in the wink of an eye,
Painted stations whistle by.
Here is a child who clambers and scrambles,
All by himself and gathering brambles;
Here is a tramp who stands and gazes;
And there is the green for stringing the daisies
Here is a cart run away in the road
Lumping along with man and load;
And here is a mill, and there is a river:
Each a glimpse and gone for ever!

WINTER-TIME

Late lies the wintry sun a-bed,
A frosty, fiery sleepy-head;
Blinks but an hour or two; and then,
A bloodred orange, sets again.
Before the stars have left the skies,
At morning in the dark I rise;
And shivering in my nakedness,
By the cold candle, bathe and dress.
Close by the jolly fire I sit
To warm my frozen bones a bit;
Or with a reindeer-sled, explore
The colder countries round the door.
When to go out, my nurse doth wrap
Me in my comforter and cap;
The cold wind burns my face, and blows
Its frosty pepper up my nose.
Black are my steps on silver sod;
Thick blows my frosty breath abroad;
And tree and house, and hill and lake,
Are frosted like a wedding-cake.

THE HAYLOFT

Through all the pleasant meadow-side
The grass grew shoulder-high,
Till the shining scythes went far and wide
And cut it down to dry.
Those green and sweetly smelling crops
They led in waggons home;
And they piled them here in mountain tops
For mountaineers to roam.
Here is Mount Clear, Mount Rusty-Nail,
Mount Eagle and Mount High; —
The mice that in these mountains dwell,
No happier are than I!
Oh, what a joy to clamber there,
Oh, what a place for play,
With the sweet, the dim, the dusty air,

The happy hills of hay!

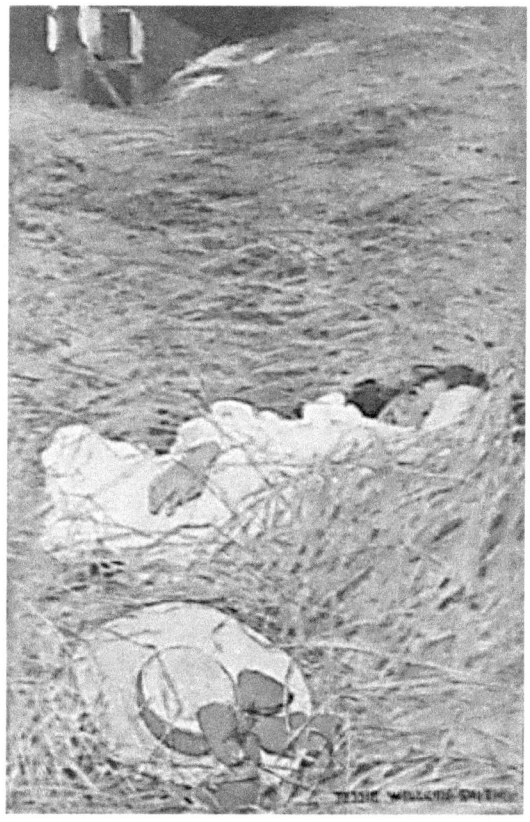

THE HAYLOFT

FAREWELL TO THE FARM

The coach is at the door at last;
The eager children, mounting fast
And kissing hands, in chorus sing:
Goodbye, goodbye, to everything!
To house and garden, field and lawn,
The meadow-gates we swang upon,
To pump and stable, tree and swing,
Goodbye, goodbye, to everything!
And fare you well for evermore,
O ladder at the hayloft door,
O hayloft where the cobwebs cling,
Goodbye, goodbye, to everything!
Crack goes the whip, and off we go;
The trees and houses smaller grow;
Last, round the woody turn we swing:
Goodbye, goodbye, to everything!

NORTHWEST PASSAGE

1. Goodnight

When the bright lamp is carried in,
The sunless hours again begin;
O'er all without, in field and lane,
The haunted night returns again.
Now we behold the embers flee
About the firelit hearth; and see
Our faces painted as we pass,
Like pictures, on the windowglass.
Must we to bed indeed? Well then,
Let us arise and go like men,
And face with an undaunted tread
The long black passage up to bed.

NORTH-WEST PASSAGE

Farewell, O brother, sister, sire!
O pleasant party round the fire!
The songs you sing, the tales you tell,
Till far tomorrow, fare ye well!

2. Shadow March

All round the house is the jet-black night;
It stares through the window-pane;
It crawls in the corners, hiding from the light,
And it moves with the moving flame.
Now my little heart goes abeating like a drum,
With the breath of the Bogie in my hair;
And all round the candle the crooked shadows come,
And go marching along up the stair.

The shadow of the balusters, the shadow of the lamp,
The shadow of the child that goes to bed —
All the wicked shadows coming, tramp, tramp, tramp,
With the black night overhead.

3. In Port

Last, to the chamber where I lie
My fearful footsteps patter nigh,
And come from out the cold and gloom
Into my warm and cheerful room.

There, safe arrived, we turn about
To keep the coming shadows out,
And close the happy door at last
On all the perils that we past.
Then, when mamma goes by to bed,
She shall come in with tip-toe tread,
And see me lying warm and fast
And in the Land of Nod at last.

THE CHILD ALONE

THE UNSEEN PLAYMATE

When children are playing alone on the green,
In comes the playmate that never was seen.
When children are happy and lonely and good,
The Friend of the Children comes out of the wood.
Nobody heard him and nobody saw,
His is a picture you never could draw,
But he's sure to be present, abroad or at home,
When children are happy and playing alone.
He lies in the laurels, he runs on the grass,
He sings when you tinkle the musical glass;
Whene'er you are happy and cannot tell why,
The Friend of the Children is sure to be by!

He loves to be little, he hates to be big,
'Tis he that inhabits the caves that you dig;
'Tis he when you play with your soldiers of tin
That sides with the Frenchmen and never can win.
'Tis he, when at night you go off to your bed,
Bids you go to your sleep and not trouble your head;
For wherever they're lying, in cupboard or shelf,
'Tis he will take care of your playthings himself!

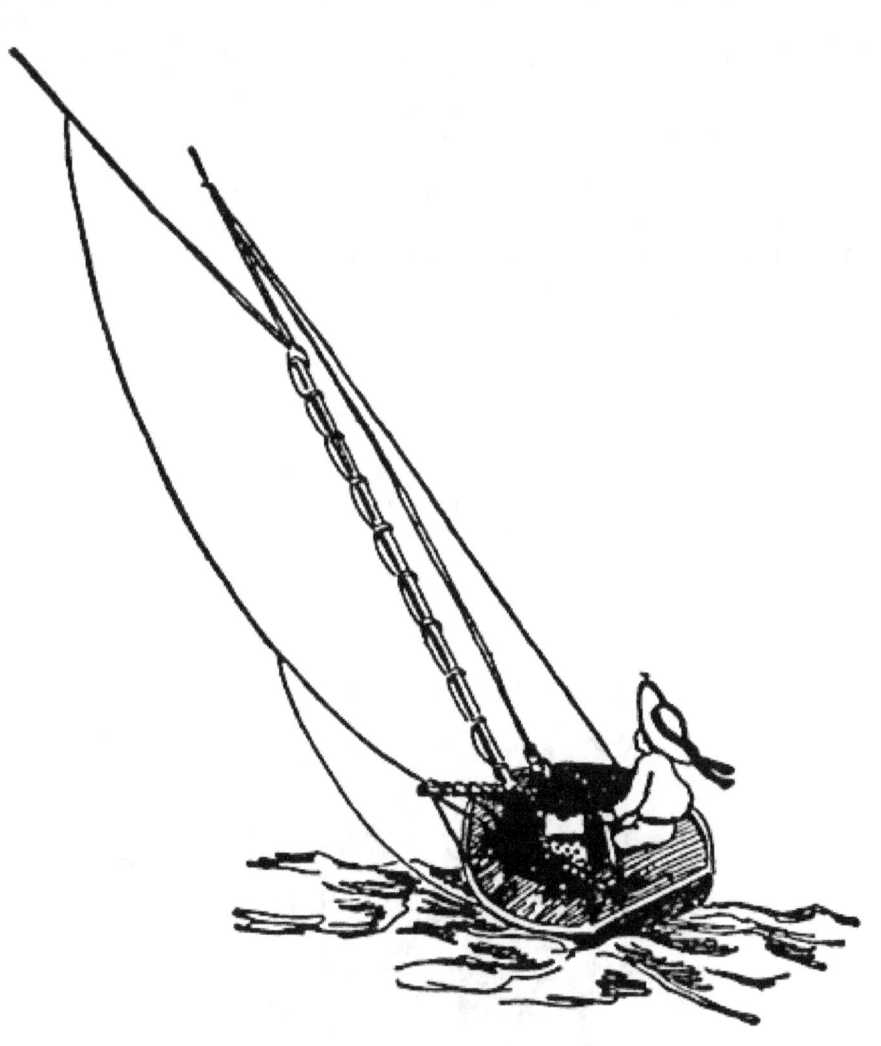

MY SHIP AND I

O it's I that am the captain of a tidy little ship,
Of a ship that goes a-sailing on the pond;
And my ship it keeps aturning all around and all about;
But when I'm a little older, I shall find the secret out
How to send my vessel sailing on beyond.
For I mean to grow as little as the dolly at the helm,
And the dolly I intend to come alive;
And with him beside to help me, it's a-sailing I shall go,
It's a-sailing on the water, when the jolly breezes blow
And the vessel goes a divie-divie-dive.

O it's then you'll see me sailing through the rushes and the reeds,
And you'll hear the water singing at the prow;
For beside the dolly sailor, I'm to voyage and explore,
To land upon the island where no dolly was before,
And to fire the penny cannon in the bow.

MY KINGDOM

Down by a shining water well
I found a very little dell,
  No higher than my head.
The heather and the gorse about
In summer bloom were coming out,
  Some yellow and some red.

I called the little pool a sea;
The little hills were big to me;
  For I am very small.
I made a boat, I made a town,
I searched the caverns up and down,
  And named them one and all.
And all about was mine, I said,
The little sparrows overhead,
  The little minnows too.
This was the world and I was king;
For me the bees came by to sing,
  For me the swallows flew.
I played there were no deeper seas,
Nor any wider plains than these,
  Nor other kings than me.
At last I heard my mother call
Out from the house at evenfall,
  To call me home to tea.
And I must rise and leave my dell,
And leave my dimpled water well,
  And leave my heather blooms.
Alas! and as my home I neared,
How very big my nurse appeared.
  How great and cool the rooms!

PICTURE-BOOKS IN WINTER

Summer fading, winter comes —
Frosty mornings, tingling thumbs,
Window robins, winter rooks,
And the picture storybooks.
Water now is turned to stone
Nurse and I can walk upon;
Still we find the flowing brooks
In the picture storybooks.
All the pretty things put by,
Wait upon the children's eye,
Sheep and shepherds, trees and crooks,
In the picture storybooks.
We may see how all things are,
Seas and cities, near and far,
And the flying fairies' looks,
In the picture storybooks.
How am I to sing your praise,
Happy chimney-corner days,
Sitting safe in nursery nooks,

Reading picture storybooks?

PICTURE-BOOKS IN WINTER

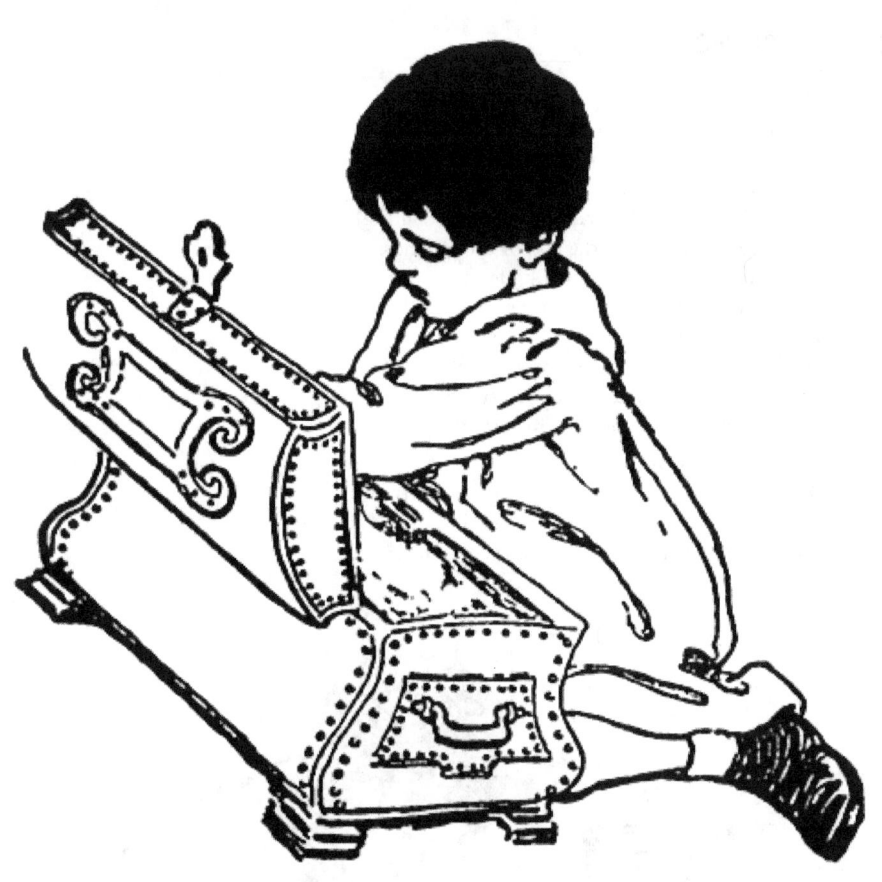

MY TREASURES

These nuts, that I keep in the back of the nest
Where all my lead soldiers are lying at rest,
Were gathered in autumn by nursie and me
In a wood with a well by the side of the sea.
This whistle we made (and how clearly it sounds!)
By the side of a field at the end of the grounds.
Of a branch of a plane, with a knife of my own,
It was nursie who made it, and nursie alone!
The stone, with the white and the yellow and grey,
We discovered I cannot tell *how* far away;
And I carried it back although weary and cold,
For though father denies it, I'm sure it is gold.

But of all my treasures the last is the king,
For there's very few children possess such a thing;
And that is a chisel, both handle and blade,
Which a man who was really a carpenter made.

BLOCK CITY

What are you able to build with your blocks?
Castles and palaces, temples and docks.
Rain may keep raining, and others go roam,
But I can be happy and building at home.
Let the sofa be mountains, the carpet be sea,
There I'll establish a city for me:
A kirk and a mill and a palace beside,
And a harbour as well where my vessels may ride.
Great is the palace with pillar and wall,
A sort of a tower on the top of it all,
And steps coming down in an orderly way
To where my toy vessels lie safe in the bay.

This one is sailing and that one is moored:
Hark to the song of the sailors on board!
And see, on the steps of my palace, the kings
Coming and going with presents and things!
Now I have done with it, down let it go!
All in a moment the town is laid low.
Block upon block lying scattered and free,
What is there left of my town by the sea?
Yet as I saw it, I see it again,
The kirk and the palace, the ships and the men,
And as long as I live and where'er I may be,
I'll always remember my town by the sea.

THE LAND OF STORYBOOKS

At evening when the lamp is lit,
Around the fire my parents sit;
They sit at home and talk and sing,
And do not play at anything.
Now, with my little gun, I crawl
All in the dark along the wall,
And follow round the forest track
Away behind the sofa back.
There, in the night, where none can spy,
All in my hunter's camp I lie,
And play at books that I have read
Till it is time to go to bed.
These are the hills, these are the woods,
These are my starry solitudes;
And there the river by whose brink
The roaring lions come to drink.

I see the others far away
As if in firelit camp they lay,
And I, like to an Indian scout,
Around their party prowled about.
So, when my nurse comes in for me,
Home I return across the sea,
And go to bed with backward looks
At my dear land of Storybooks.

ARMIES IN THE FIRE

The lamps now glitter down the street;
Faintly sound the falling feet;
And the blue even slowly falls
About the garden trees and walls.
Now in the falling of the gloom
The red fire paints the empty room:
And warmly on the roof it looks,
And flickers on the backs of books.
Armies march by tower and spire
Of cities blazing, in the fire; —
Till as I gaze with staring eyes,
The armies fade, the lustre dies.
Then once again the glow returns;
Again the phantom city burns;
And down the red-hot valley, lo!
The phantom armies marching go!

Blinking embers, tell me true
Where are those armies marching to,
And what the burning city is
That crumbles in your furnaces!

THE LITTLE LAND

When at home alone I sit,
And am very tired of it,
I have just to shut my eyes
To go sailing through the skies —
To go sailing far away
To the pleasant Land of Play;
To the fairy land afar
Where the Little People are;
Where the clover-tops are trees,
And the rain-pools are the seas,
And the leaves, like little ships,
Sail about on tiny trips;
And above the daisy tree
Through the grasses,
High o'erhead the Bumble Bee
Hums and passes.
In that forest to and fro
I can wander, I can go;
See the spider and the fly,
And the ants go marching by,
Carrying parcels with their feet
Down the green and grassy street.
I can in the sorrel sit
Where the ladybird alit.
I can climb the jointed grass
And on high
See the greater swallows pass
In the sky,
And the round sun rolling by
Heeding no such things as I.
Through that forest I can pass
Till, as in a looking-glass,
Humming fly and daisy tree
And my tiny self I see,
Painted very clear and neat
On the rain-pool at my feet.
Should a leaflet come to land
Drifting near to where I stand,
Straight I'll board that tiny boat
Round the rain-pool sea to float.

Little thoughtful creatures sit
On the grassy coasts of it;
Little things with lovely eyes
See me sailing with surprise.
Some are clad in armour green —
(These have sure to battle been!) —
Some are pied with ev'ry hue,
Black and crimson, gold and blue;
Some have wings and swift are gone; —
But they all look kindly on.

THE LITTLE LAND

When my eyes I once again
Open, and see all things plain:
High bare walls, great bare floor;
Great big knobs on drawer and door;
Great big people perched on chairs,
Stitching tucks and mending tears,

Each a hill that I could climb,
And talking nonsense all the time —
O dear me,
That I could be
A sailor on the rain-pool sea,
A climber in the clover tree,
And just come back, a sleepy-head,
Late at night to go to bed.

GARDEN DAYS

NIGHT AND DAY

When the golden day is done,
Through the closing portal,
Child and garden, flower and sun,
Vanish all things mortal.
As the blinding shadows fall
As the rays diminish,
Under evening's cloak, they all
Roll away and vanish.
Garden darkened, daisy shut,
Child in bed, they slumber —
Glowworm in the highway rut,
Mice among the lumber.
In the darkness houses shine,
Parents move with candles;

Till on all, the night divine
Turns the bedroom handles.

Till at last the day begins
In the east a-breaking,
In the hedges and the whins
Sleeping birds awaking.
In the darkness shapes of things,
Houses, trees and hedges,
Clearer grow; and sparrow's wings
Beat on window ledges.
These shall wake the yawning maid;
She the door shall open —
Finding dew on garden glade
And the morning broken.
There my garden grows again
Green and rosy painted,
As at eve behind the pane
From my eyes it fainted.
Just as it was shut away,
Toy-like, in the even,
Here I see it glow with day
Under glowing heaven.
Every path and every plot,
Every bush of roses,
Every blue forget-me-not
Where the dew reposes.

"Up!" they cry, "the day is come
On the smiling valleys:
We have beat the morning drum;
Playmate, join your allies!"

NEST EGGS

Birds all the sunny day
Flutter and quarrel
Here in the arbour-like
Tent of the laurel.
Here in the fork
The brown nest is seated;
Four little blue eggs
The mother keeps heated.
While we stand watching her
Staring like gabies,
Safe in each egg are the
Bird's little babies.
Soon the frail eggs they shall
Chip, and upspringing
Make all the April woods
Merry with singing.

Younger than we are,
O children, and frailer,
Soon in blue air they'll be,
Singer and sailor.
We, so much older,
Taller and stronger,
We shall look down on the
Birdies no longer.
They shall go flying
With musical speeches
High over head in the
Tops of the beeches.
In spite of our wisdom
And sensible talking,
We on our feet must go
Plodding and walking.

THE FLOWERS

All the names I know from nurse:
Gardener's garters, Shepherd's purse,
Bachelor's buttons, Lady's smock,
And the Lady Hollyhock.
Fairy places, fairy things,
Fairy woods where the wild bee wings,
Tiny trees for tiny dames —
These must all be fairy names!
Tiny woods below whose boughs
Shady fairies weave a house;
Tiny treetops, rose or thyme,
Where the braver fairies climb!

THE FLOWERS

Fair are grown-up people's trees,
But the fairest woods are these;

Where, if I were not so tall,
I should live for good and all.

SUMMER SUN

Great is the sun, and wide he goes
Through empty heaven without repose;
And in the blue and glowing days
More thick than rain he showers his rays.
Though closer still the blinds we pull
To keep the shady parlour cool,
Yet he will find a chink or two
To slip his golden fingers through.
The dusty attic spider-clad
He, through the keyhole, maketh glad;
And through the broken edge of tiles
Into the laddered hayloft smiles.
Meantime his golden face around
He bares to all the garden ground,
And sheds a warm and glittering look
Among the ivy's inmost nook.
Above the hills, along the blue,
Round the bright air with footing true,
To please the child, to paint the rose,
The gardener of the World, he goes.

THE DUMB SOLDIER

When the grass was closely mown,
Walking on the lawn alone,
In the turf a hole I found,
And hid a soldier underground.
Spring and daisies came apace;
Grasses hide my hiding place;
Grasses run like a green sea
O'er the lawn up to my knee.
Under grass alone he lies,
Looking up with leaden eyes,
Scarlet coat and pointed gun,
To the stars and to the sun.
When the grass is ripe like grain,
When the scythe is stoned again,
When the lawn is shaven clear,
Then my hole shall reappear.
I shall find him, never fear,
I shall find my grenadier;
But for all that's gone and come,
I shall find my soldier dumb.
He has lived, a little thing,
In the grassy woods of spring;
Done, if he could tell me true,
Just as I should like to do.

He has seen the starry hours
And the springing of the flowers;
And the fairy things that pass
In the forests of the grass.
In the silence he has heard
Talking bee and ladybird,
And the butterfly has flown
O'er him as he lay alone.
Not a word will he disclose,
Not a word of all he knows.
I must lay him on the shelf,
And make up the tale myself.

AUTUMN FIRES

In the other gardens
And all up the vale,
From the autumn bonfires
See the smoke trail!
Pleasant summer over
And all the summer flowers,
The red fire blazes,
The grey smoke towers.
Sing a song of seasons!
Something bright in all!
Flowers in the summer,
Fires in the fall!

THE GARDENER

The gardener does not love to talk,
He makes me keep the gravel walk;
And when he puts his tools away,
He locks the door and takes the key.
Away behind the currant row,
Where no one else but cook may go,
Far in the plots, I see him dig,
Old and serious, brown and big.
He digs the flowers, green, red, and blue,
Nor wishes to be spoken to.
He digs the flowers and cuts the hay,
And never seems to want to play.

Silly gardener! summer goes,
And winter comes with pinching toes,
When in the garden bare and brown
You must lay your barrow down.
Well now, and while the summer stays,
To profit by these garden days
O how much wiser you would be
To play at Indian wars with me!

HISTORICAL ASSOCIATIONS

Dear Uncle Jim, this garden ground
That now you smoke your pipe around,
Has seen immortal actions done
And valiant battles lost and won.
Here we had best on tip-toe tread,
While I for safety march ahead,
For this is that enchanted ground
Where all who loiter slumber sound.

Here is the sea, here is the sand,
Here is simple Shepherd's Land,
Here are the fairy hollyhocks,
And there are Ali Baba's rocks.
But yonder, see! apart and high,
Frozen Siberia lies; where I,
With Robert Bruce and William Tell,
Was bound by an enchanter's spell.

ENVOYS

TO WILLIE AND HENRIETTA

If two may read aright
These rhymes of old delight
And house and garden play,
You too, my cousins, and you only, may.
You in a garden green
With me were king and queen,
Were hunter, soldier, tar,
And all the thousand things that children are.
Now in the elders' seat
We rest with quiet feet,
And from the window-bay
We watch the children, our successors, play.
"Time was," the golden head
Irrevocably said;
But time which none can bind,
While flowing fast away, leaves love behind.

TO MY MOTHER

You too, my mother, read my rhymes
For love of unforgotten times,
And you may chance to hear once more
The little feet along the floor.

TO AUNTIE

Chief of our aunts — not only I,
But all your dozen of nurselings cry —
What did the other children do?

And what were childhood, wanting you?

TO AUNTIE

TO MINNIE

The red room with the giant bed
Where none but elders laid their head;
The little room where you and I
Did for awhile together lie
And, simple suitor, I your hand
In decent marriage did demand;
The great day nursery, best of all,
With pictures pasted on the wall
And leaves upon the blind
A pleasant room wherein to wake
And hear the leafy garden shake
And rustle in the wind —
And pleasant there to lie in bed
And see the pictures overhead —
The wars about Sebastopol,
The grinning guns along the wall,
The daring escalade,
The plunging ships, the bleating sheep,
The happy children ankle-deep
And laughing as they wade;
All these are vanished clean away,
And the old manse is changed to-day;
It wears an altered face

And shields a stranger race.
The river, on from mill to mill,
Flows past our childhood's garden still;
But ah! we children never more
Shall watch it from the water-door.
Below the yew — it still is there —
Our phantom voices haunt the air
As we were still at play,
And I can hear them call and say:
"*How far is it to Babylon?*"

Ah, far enough, my dear,
Far, far enough from here —
Yet you have farther gone!
"*Can I get there by candlelight?*"
So goes the old refrain.
I do not know — perchance you might —
But only, children, hear it right,
Ah, never to return again!
The eternal dawn, beyond a doubt,
Shall break on hill and plain,
And put all stars and candles out
Ere we be young again.

To you in distant India, these
I send across the seas,
Nor count it far across.
For which of us forgets
The Indian cabinets,

The bones of antelope, the wings of albatross,
The pied and painted birds and beans,
The junks and bangles, beads and screens,
The gods and sacred bells,
And the loud-humming, twisting shells!
The level of the parlour floor
Was honest, homely, Scottish shore;
But when we climbed upon a chair,
Behold the gorgeous East was there!
Be this a fable; and behold
Me in the parlour as of old,
And Minnie just above me set
In the quaint Indian cabinet!
Smiling and kind, you grace a shelf
Too high for me to reach myself.
Reach down a hand, my dear, and take
These rhymes for old acquaintance' sake!

TO MY NAME-CHILD

1

Some day soon this rhyming volume, if you learn with proper speed,
Little Louis Sanchez, will be given you to read.
Then shall you discover, that your name was printed down
By the English printers, long before, in London town.
In the great and busy city where the East and West are met,
All the little letters did the English printer set;
While you thought of nothing, and were still too young to play,
Foreign people thought of you in places far away.
Ay, and while you slept, a baby, over all the English lands
Other little children took the volume in their hands;
Other children questioned, in their homes across the seas:
Who was little Louis, won't you tell us, mother, please?

2

Now that you have spelt your lesson, lay it down and go and play,
Seeking shells and seaweed on the sands of Monterey,
Watching all the mighty whalebones, lying buried by the breeze,
Tiny sandpipers, and the huge Pacific seas.
And remember in your playing, as the sea-fog rolls to you,
Long ere you could read it, how I told you what to do;
And that while you thought of no one, nearly half the world away
Some one thought of Louis on the beach of Monterey!

TO ANY READER

As from the house your mother sees
You playing round the garden trees,
So you may see, if you will look
Through the windows of this book,
Another child, far, far away,
And in another garden, play.
But do not think you can at all,
By knocking on the window, call
That child to hear you. He intent
Is all on his play-business bent.
He does not hear; he will not look,
Nor yet be lured out of this book.
For, long ago, the truth to say,
He has grown up and gone away,
And it is but a child of air
That lingers in the garden there.

UNDERWOODS

Of all my verse, like not a single line;
But like my title, for it is not mine.
That title from a better man I stole;
Ah, how much better, had I stol'n the whole!

DEDICATION

There are men and classes of men that stand above the common herd: the soldier, the sailor, and the shepherd not unfrequently; the artist rarely; rarelier still, the clergyman; the physician almost as a rule. He is the flower (such as it is) of our civilisation; and when that stage of man is done with, and only remembered to be marvelled at in history, he will be thought to have shared as little as any in the defects of the period, and most notably exhibited the virtues of the race. Generosity he has, such as is possible to those who practise an art, never to those who drive a trade; discretion, tested by a hundred secrets; tact, tried in a thousand embarrassments; and, what are more important, Heraclean cheerfulness and courage. So it is that he brings air and cheer into the sickroom, and often enough, though not so often as he wishes, brings healing.

Gratitude is but a lame sentiment; thanks, when they are expressed, are often more embarrassing than welcome; and yet I must set forth mine to a few out of many doctors who have brought me comfort and help: to Dr. Willey of San Francisco, whose kindness to a stranger it must be as grateful to him, as it is touching to me, to remember; to Dr. Karl Ruedi of Davos, the good genius of the English in his frosty mountains; to Dr. Herbert of Paris, whom I knew only for a week, and to Dr. Caissot of Montpellier, whom I knew only for ten days, and who have yet written their names deeply in my memory; to Dr. Brandt of Royat; to Dr. Wakefield of Nice; to Dr. Chepmell, whose visits make it a pleasure to be ill; to Dr. Horace Dobell, so wise in counsel; to Sir Andrew Clark, so unwearied in kindness; and to that wise youth, my uncle, Dr. Balfour.

I forget as many as I remember; and I ask both to pardon me, these for silence, those for inadequate speech. But one name I have kept on purpose to the last, because it is a household word with me, and because if I had not received favours from so many hands and in so many quarters of the world, it should have stood upon this page alone: that of my friend Thomas Bodley Scott of Bournemouth. Will he accept this, although shared among so many, for a dedication to himself? and when next my ill-fortune (which has thus its pleasant side) brings him hurrying to me when he would fain sit down to meat or lie down to rest, will he care to remember that he takes this trouble for one who is not fool enough to be ungrateful?

R. L. S.

BOOK I

IN ENGLISH

ENVOY

Go, little book, and wish to all
Flowers in the garden, meat in the hall,
A bin of wine, a spice of wit,
A house with lawns enclosing it,
A living river by the door,
A nightingale in the sycamore!

A SONG OF THE ROAD

The gauger walked with willing foot,
And aye the gauger played the flute;
And what should Master Gauger play
But *Over the hills and far away*?
Whene'er I buckle on my pack
And foot it gaily in the track,
O pleasant gauger, long since dead,
I hear you fluting on ahead.
You go with me the selfsame way —
The selfsame air for me you play;
For I do think and so do you
It is the tune to travel to.

For who would gravely set his face
To go to this or t'other place?
There's nothing under heav'n so blue
That's fairly worth the travelling to.
On every hand the roads begin,
And people walk with zeal therein;
But wheresoe'er the highways tend,
Be sure there's nothing at the end.
Then follow you, wherever hie
The travelling mountains of the sky.
Or let the streams in civil mode
Direct your choice upon a road;
For one and all, or high or low,
Will lead you where you wish to go;
And one and all go night and day
Over the hills and far away!
Forest of Montargis.

THE CANOE SPEAKS

On the great streams the ships may go
About men's business to and fro.
But I, the eggshell pinnace, sleep
On crystal waters ankle-deep:
I, whose diminutive design,
Of sweeter cedar, pithier pine,
Is fashioned on so frail a mould,
A hand may launch, a hand withhold:

I, rather, with the leaping trout
Wind, among lilies, in and out;
I, the unnamed, inviolate,
Green, rustic rivers navigate;
My dipping paddle scarcely shakes
The berry in the bramble-brakes;
Still forth on my green way I wend
Beside the cottage garden-end;
And by the nested angler fare,
And take the lovers unaware.
By willow wood and water-wheel
Speedily fleets my touching keel;
By all retired and shady spots
Where prosper dim forget-me-nots;
By meadows where at afternoon
The growing maidens troop in June
To loose their girdles on the grass.
Ah! speedier than before the glass
The backward toilet goes; and swift
As swallows quiver, robe and shift
And the rough country stockings lie
Around each young divinity.
When, following the recondite brook,
Sudden upon this scene I look,
And light with unfamiliar face
On chaste Diana's bathing-place,
Loud ring the hills about and all
The shallows are abandoned....

It is the season now to go
About the country high and low,
Among the lilacs hand in hand,
And two by two in fairyland.
The brooding boy, the sighing maid,
Wholly fain and half afraid,
Now meet along the hazel'd brook
To pass and linger, pause and look.
A year ago, and blithely paired,
Their rough-and-tumble play they shared;
They kissed and quarrelled, laughed and cried,
A year ago at Eastertide.
With bursting heart, with fiery face,
She strove against him in the race;

He unabashed her garter saw,
That now would touch her skirts with awe.
Now by the stile ablaze she stops,
And his demurer eyes he drops;
Now they exchange averted sighs
Or stand and marry silent eyes.
And he to her a hero is
And sweeter she than primroses;
Their common silence dearer far
Than nightingale and mavis are.
Now when they sever wedded hands,
Joy trembles in their bosom-strands
And lovely laughter leaps and falls
Upon their lips in madrigals.

THE HOUSE BEAUTIFUL

A naked house, a naked moor,
A shivering pool before the door,
A garden bare of flowers and fruit
And poplars at the garden foot:
Such is the place that I live in,
Bleak without and bare within.
Yet shall your ragged moor receive
The incomparable pomp of eve,
And the cold glories of the dawn
Behind your shivering trees be drawn;
And when the wind from place to place
Doth the unmoored cloud-galleons chase,
Your garden gloom and gleam again,
With leaping sun, with glancing rain.
Here shall the wizard moon ascend
The heavens, in the crimson end
Of day's declining splendour; here
The army of the stars appear.
The neighbour hollows, dry or wet,
Spring shall with tender flowers beset;
And oft the morning muser see
Larks rising from the broomy lea,
And every fairy wheel and thread
Of cobweb, dew-bediamonded.
When daisies go, shall winter-time
Silver the simple grass with rime;
Autumnal frosts enchant the pool
And make the cart-ruts beautiful;
And when snow-bright the moor expands,
How shall your children clap their hands!

To make this earth, our hermitage,
A cheerful and a changeful page,
God's bright and intricate device
Of days and seasons doth suffice.

A VISIT FROM THE SEA

Far from the loud sea beaches
Where he goes fishing and crying,
Here in the inland garden
Why is the seagull flying?
Here are no fish to dive for;
Here is the corn and lea;
Here are the green trees rustling.
Hie away home to sea!
Fresh is the river water
And quiet among the rushes;
This is no home for the seagull,
But for the rooks and thrushes.
Pity the bird that has wandered!
Pity the sailor ashore!
Hurry him home to the ocean,
Let him come here no more!
High on the sea-cliff ledges
The white gulls are trooping and crying,
Here among rooks and roses,
Why is the seagull flying?

TO A GARDENER

Friend, in my mountainside demesne,
My plain-beholding, rosy, green
And linnet-haunted garden-ground,
Let still the esculents abound.
Let first the onion flourish there,
Rose among roots, the maiden-fair,
Wine-scented and poetic soul
Of the capacious salad-bowl.
Let thyme the mountaineer (to dress
The tinier birds) and wading cress,
The lover of the shallow brook,
From all my plots and borders look.
Nor crisp and ruddy radish, nor
Pease-cods for the child's pinafore
Be lacking; nor of salad clan
The last and least that ever ran
About great nature's garden-beds.
Nor thence be missed the speary heads
Of artichoke; nor thence the bean
That gathered innocent and green
Outsavours the belauded pea.
These tend, I prithee; and for me,
Thy most longsuffering master, bring
In April, when the linnets sing
And the days lengthen more and more,
At sundown to the garden door.
And I, being provided thus,
Shall, with superb asparagus,
A book, a taper, and a cup
Of country wine, divinely sup.
La Solitude, Hyères.

TO MINNIE

(WITH A HAND-GLASS)

A picture-frame for you to fill,
A paltry setting for your face,
A thing that has no worth until
You lend it something of your grace,
I send (unhappy I that sing
Laid by a while upon the shelf)
Because I would not send a thing
Less charming than you are yourself.
And happier than I, alas!
(Dumb thing, I envy its delight)
'Twill wish you well, the looking-glass,
And look you in the face tonight.

TO K. de M.

A lover of the moorland bare
And honest country winds you were;
The silver-skimming rain you took;
And love the floodings of the brook,
Dew, frost and mountains, fire and seas,
Tumultuary silences,
Winds that in darkness fifed a tune,
And the high-riding, virgin moon.

And as the berry, pale and sharp,
Springs on some ditch's counterscarp
In our ungenial, native north —
You put your frosted wildings forth,
And on the heath, afar from man,
A strong and bitter virgin ran.
The berry ripened keeps the rude
And racy flavour of the wood.
And you that loved the empty plain
All redolent of wind and rain,
Around you still the curlew sings —
The freshness of the weather clings —
The maiden jewels of the rain
Sit in your dabbled locks again.

TO N. V. de G. S.

The unfathomable sea, and time, and tears,
The deeds of heroes and the crimes of kings
Dispart us; and the river of events
Has, for an age of years, to east and west
More widely borne our cradles. Thou to me
Art foreign, as when seamen at the dawn
Descry a land far off, and know not which.
So I approach uncertain; so I cruise
Round thy mysterious islet, and behold
Surf and great mountains and loud river-bars,
And from the shore hear inland voices call.
Strange is the seaman's heart; he hopes, he fears;
Draws closer and sweeps wider from that coast;
Last, his rent sail refits, and to the deep
His shattered prow uncomforted puts back.

Yet as he goes he ponders at the helm
Of that bright island; where he feared to touch,
His spirit re-adventures; and for years,
Where by his wife he slumbers safe at home,
Thoughts of that land revisit him; he sees
The eternal mountains beckon, and awakes
Yearning for that far home that might have been.

TO WILL. H. LOW

Youth now flees on feathered foot,
Faint and fainter sounds the flute,
Rarer songs of gods; and still
Somewhere on the sunny hill,
Or along the winding stream,
Through the willows, flits a dream;
Flits but shows a smiling face,
Flees, but with so quaint a grace,
None can choose to stay at home,
All must follow, all must roam.
This is unborn beauty: she
Now in air floats high and free.
Takes the sun and makes the blue; —
Late with stooping pinion flew
Raking hedgerow trees, and wet
Her wing in silver streams, and set
Shining foot on temple roof:
Now again she flies aloof,
Coasting mountain clouds and kiss't
By the evening's amethyst.
In wet wood and miry lane,
Still we pant and pound in vain;

Still with leaden foot we chase
Waning pinion, fainting face;
Still with grey hair we stumble on,
Till, behold, the vision gone!
Where hath fleeting beauty led?
To the doorway of the dead.
Life is over, life was gay:
We have come the primrose way.

TO MRS. WILL. H. LOW

    Even in the bluest noonday of July,
There could not run the smallest breath of wind
But all the quarter sounded like a wood;
And in the chequered silence and above
The hum of city cabs that sought the Bois,
Suburban ashes shivered into song.
A patter and a chatter and a chirp
And a long dying hiss — it was as though
Starched old brocaded dames through all the house
Had trailed a strident skirt, or the whole sky
Even in a wink had over-brimmed in rain.
Hark, in these shady parlours, how it talks
Of the near Autumn, how the smitten ash
Trembles and augurs floods! O not too long
In these inconstant latitudes delay,
O not too late from the unbeloved north
Trim your escape! For soon shall this low roof
Resound indeed with rain, soon shall your eyes
Search the foul garden, search the darkened rooms,
Nor find one jewel but the blazing log.
Rue Vernier, Paris.

TO H. F. BROWN

(WRITTEN DURING A DANGEROUS SICKNESS)

I sit and wait a pair of oars
On cis-Elysian river-shores.
Where the immortal dead have sate,
'Tis mine to sit and meditate;
To reascend life's rivulet,
Without remorse, without regret;
And sing my *Alma Genetrix*
Among the willows of the Styx.
And lo, as my serener soul
Did these unhappy shores patrol,
And wait with an attentive ear
The coming of the gondolier,
Your fire-surviving roll I took,
Your spirited and happy book;
Whereon, despite my frowning fate,
It did my soul so recreate
That all my fancies fled away
On a Venetian holiday.
Now, thanks to your triumphant care,
Your pages clear as April air,
The sails, the bells, the birds, I know,
And the far-off Friulan snow;
The land and sea, the sun and shade,
And the blue even lamp-inlaid.

For this, for these, for all, O friend,
For your whole book from end to end —
For Paron Piero's mutton-ham —
I your defaulting debtor am.
Perchance, reviving, yet may I
To your sea-paven city hie,
And in a *felze* some day yet
Light at your pipe my cigarette.

TO ANDREW LANG

Dear Andrew, with the brindled hair,
Who glory to have thrown in air,
High over arm, the trembling reed,
By Ale and Kail, by Till and Tweed:
An equal craft of hand you show
The pen to guide, the fly to throw:
I count you happy-starred; for God,
When He with inkpot and with rod
Endowed you, bade your fortune lead
For ever by the crooks of Tweed,
For ever by the woods of song
And lands that to the Muse belong;
Or if in peopled streets, or in
The abhorred pedantic sanhedrin,
It should be yours to wander, still
Airs of the morn, airs of the hill,
The plovery Forest and the seas
That break about the Hebrides,
Should follow over field and plain
And find you at the window-pane;

And you again see hill and peel,
And the bright springs gush at your heel.
So went the fiat forth, and so
Garrulous like a brook you go,
With sound of happy mirth and sheen
Of daylight — whether by the green
You fare that moment, or the grey;
Whether you dwell in March or May;
Or whether treat of reels and rods
Or of the old unhappy gods:
Still like a brook your page has shone,
And your ink sings of Helicon.

ET TU IN ARCADIA VIXISTI

(TO R. A. M. S.)

In ancient tales, O friend, thy spirit dwelt;
There, from of old, thy childhood passed; and there
High expectation, high delights and deeds,
Thy fluttering heart with hope and terror moved.
And thou hast heard of yore the Blatant Beast,
And Roland's horn, and that war-scattering shout
Of all-unarmed Achilles, ægis-crowned.
And perilous lands thou sawest, sounding shores
And seas and forests drear, island and dale
And mountain dark. For thou with Tristram rod'st
Or Bedevere, in farthest Lyonesse.
Thou hadst a booth in Samarcand, whereat
Side-looking Magians trafficked; thence, by night,
An Afreet snatched thee, and with wings upbore
Beyond the Aral Mount; or, hoping gain,
Thou, with a jar of money, didst embark

For Balsorah by sea. But chiefly thou
In that clear air took'st life; in Arcady
The haunted, land of song; and by the wells
Where most the gods frequent. There Chiron old,
In the Pelethronian antre, taught thee lore;
The plants he taught, and by the shining stars
In forests dim to steer. There hast thou seen
Immortal Pan dance secret in a glade,
And, dancing, roll his eyes; these, where they fell,
Shed glee, and through the congregated oaks
A flying horror winged; while all the earth
To the god's pregnant footing thrilled within.
Or whiles, beside the sobbing stream, he breathed,
In his clutched pipe unformed and wizard strains
Divine yet brutal; which the forest heard,
And thou, with awe; and far upon the plain
The unthinking ploughman started and gave ear.
Now things there are that, upon him who sees,
A strong vocation lay; and strains there are
That whoso hears shall hear for evermore.
For evermore thou hear'st immortal Pan
And those melodious godheads, ever young
And ever quiring, on the mountains old.
What was this earth, child of the gods, to thee?
Forth from thy dreamland thou, a dreamer, cam'st
And in thine ears the olden music rang,
And in thy mind the doings of the dead,
And those heroic ages long forgot.
To a so fallen earth, alas! too late,
Alas! in evil days, thy steps return,
To list at noon for nightingales, to grow
A dweller on the beach till Argo come

That came long since, a lingerer by the pool
Where that desirèd angel bathes no more.

As when the Indian to Dakota comes,
Or farthest Idaho, and where he dwelt,
He with his clan, a humming city finds;
Thereon a while, amazed, he stares, and then
To right and leftward, like a questing dog,
Seeks first the ancestral altars, then the hearth
Long cold with rains, and where old terror lodged,
And where the dead: so thee undying Hope,
With all her pack, hunts screaming through the years:
Here, there, thou fleeëst; but nor here nor there
The pleasant gods abide, the glory dwells.
That, that was not Apollo, not the god.
This was not Venus, though she Venus seemed
A moment. And though fair yon river move,
She, all the way, from disenchanted fount
To seas unhallowed runs; the gods forsook
Long since her trembling rushes; from her plains
Disconsolate, long since adventure fled;
And now although the inviting river flows,
And every poplared cape, and every bend
Or willowy islet, win upon thy soul
And to thy hopeful shallop whisper speed;
Yet hope not thou at all; hope is no more;
And O, long since the golden groves are dead
The faëry cities vanished from the land!

TO W.E. HENLEY

The year runs through her phases; rain and sun,
Springtime and summer pass; winter succeeds;
But one pale season rules the house of death.
Cold falls the imprisoned daylight; fell disease

By each lean pallet squats, and pain and sleep
Toss gaping on the pillows.
But O thou!
Uprise and take thy pipe. Bid music flow,
Strains by good thoughts attended, like the spring
The swallows follow over land and sea.
Pain sleeps at once; at once, with open eyes,
Dozing despair awakes. The shepherd sees
His flock come bleating home; the seaman hears
Once more the cordage rattle. Airs of home!
Youth, love, and roses blossom; the gaunt ward
Dislimns and disappears, and, opening out,
Shows brooks and forests, and the blue beyond
Of mountains.
Small the pipe; but O! do thou,
Peak-faced and suffering piper, blow therein
The dirge of heroes dead; and to these sick,
These dying, sound the triumph over death.
Behold! each greatly breathes; each tastes a joy
Unknown before, in dying; for each knows
A hero dies with him — though unfulfilled,
Yet conquering truly — and not dies in vain.
So is pain cheered, death comforted; the house
Of sorrow smiles to listen. Once again —
O thou, Orpheus and Heracles, the bard
And the deliverer, touch the stops again!

HENRY JAMES

Who comes tonight? We ope the doors in vain.
Who comes? My bursting walls, can you contain
The presences that now together throng
Your narrow entry, as with flowers and song,

As with the air of life, the breath of talk?
Lo, how these fair immaculate women walk
Behind their jocund maker; and we see
Slighted *De Mauves*, and that far different she,
Gressie, the trivial sphynx; and to our feast
Daisy and *Barb* and *Chancellor* (she not least!)
With all their silken, all their airy kin,
Do like unbidden angels enter in.
But he, attended by these shining names,
Comes (best of all) himself — our welcome James.

THE MIRROR SPEAKS

Where the bells peal far at sea
Cunning fingers fashioned me.
There on palace walls I hung
While that Consuelo sung;
But I heard, though I listened well,
Never a note, never a trill,
Never a beat of the chiming bell.
There I hung and looked, and there
In my grey face, faces fair
Shone from under shining hair.
Well I saw the poising head,
But the lips moved and nothing said;
And when lights were in the hall,
Silent moved the dancers all.
So a while I glowed, and then
Fell on dusty days and men;
Long I slumbered packed in straw,
Long I none but dealers saw;
Till before my silent eye
One that sees came passing by.

Now with an outlandish grace,
To the sparkling fire I face
In the blue room at Skerryvore;
Where I wait until the door
Open, and the Prince of Men,
Henry James, shall come again.

KATHARINE

We see you as we see a face
That trembles in a forest place
Upon the mirror of a pool
For ever quiet, clear, and cool;
And, in the wayward glass, appears
To hover between smiles and tears,
Elfin and human, airy and true,
And backed by the reflected blue.

TO F. J. S.

I read, dear friend, in your dear face
Your life's tale told with perfect grace;
The river of your life I trace
Up the sun-chequered, devious bed
To the far-distant fountain-head.
Not one quick beat of your warm heart,
Nor thought that came to you apart,
Pleasure nor pity, love nor pain
Nor sorrow, has gone by in vain;

But as some lone, wood-wandering child
Brings home with him at evening mild
The thorns and flowers of all the wild,
From your whole life, O fair and true,
Your flowers and thorns you bring with you!

REQUIEM

Under the wide and starry sky,
Dig the grave and let me lie.
Glad did I live and gladly die,
And I laid me down with a will.
This be the verse you grave for me:
Here he lies where he longed to be;
Home is the sailor, home from sea,
And the hunter home from the hill.
Hyères, *May.*

THE CELESTIAL SURGEON

If I have faltered more or less
In my great task of happiness;
If I have moved among my race
And shown no glorious morning face;
If beams from happy human eyes
Have moved me not; if morning skies,
Books, and my food, and summer rain
Knocked on my sullen heart in vain: —
Lord, Thy most pointed pleasure take
And stab my spirit broad awake;

Or, Lord, if too obdurate I,
Choose Thou, before that spirit die,
A piercing pain, a killing sin,
And to my dead heart run them in!

OUR LADY OF THE SNOWS

Out of the sun, out of the blast,
Out of the world, alone I passed
Across the moor and through the wood
To where the monastery stood.
There neither lute nor breathing fife,
Nor rumour of the world of life,
Nor confidences low and dear,
Shall strike the meditative ear.
Aloof, unhelpful, and unkind,
The prisoners of the iron mind,
Where nothing speaks except the bell,
The unfraternal brothers dwell.
Poor passionate men, still clothed afresh
With agonising folds of flesh;
Whom the clear eyes solicit still
To some bold output of the will,
While fairy Fancy far before
And musing Memory-Hold-the-door
Now to heroic death invite
And now uncurtain fresh delight:
O, little boots it thus to dwell
On the remote unneighboured hill!
O to be up and doing, O
Unfearing and unshamed to go

In all the uproar and the press
About my human business!
My undissuaded heart I hear
Whisper courage in my ear.
With voiceless calls, the ancient earth
Summons me to a daily birth.
Thou, O my love, ye, O my friends —
The gist of life, the end of ends —
To laugh, to love, to live, to die,
Ye call me by the ear and eye!
Forth from the casemate, on the plain
Where honour has the world to gain,
Pour forth and bravely do your part,
O knights of the unshielded heart!
Forth and for ever forward! — out
From prudent turret and redoubt,
And in the mellay charge amain,
To fall but yet to rise again!
Captive? ah, still, to honour bright,
A captive soldier of the right!
Or free and fighting, good with ill?
Unconquering but unconquered still!
And ye, O brethren, what if God,
When from Heav'n's top He spies abroad,
And sees on this tormented stage
The noble war of mankind rage:

What if His vivifying eye,
O monks, should pass your corner by?
For still the Lord is Lord of might;
In deeds, in deeds, He takes delight;
The plough, the spear, the laden barks,
The field, the founded city, marks;
He marks the smiler of the streets,
The singer upon garden seats;

He sees the climber in the rocks:
To Him, the shepherd folds his flocks.
For those He loves that underprop
With daily virtues Heaven's top,
And bear the falling sky with ease,
Unfrowning caryatides.
Those He approves that ply the trade,
That rock the child, that wed the maid,
That with weak virtues, weaker hands,
Sow gladness on the peopled lands.
And still with laughter, song and shout,
Spin the great wheel of earth about.
But ye? — O ye who linger still
Here in your fortress on the hill,
With placid face, with tranquil breath,
The unsought volunteers of death,
Our cheerful General on high
With careless looks may pass you by.

Not yet, my soul, these friendly fields desert,
Where thou with grass, and rivers, and the breeze,
And the bright face of day, thy dalliance hadst;
Where to thine ear first sang the enraptured birds;
Where love and thou that lasting bargain made.
The ship rides trimmed, and from the eternal shore
Thou hearest airy voices; but not yet
Depart, my soul, not yet a while depart.
Freedom is far, rest far. Thou art with life
Too closely woven, nerve with nerve entwined;
Service still craving service, love for love,
Love for dear love, still suppliant with tears.

Alas, not yet thy human task is done!
A bond at birth is forged; a debt doth lie
Immortal on mortality. It grows —
By vast rebound it grows, unceasing growth;
Gift upon gift, alms upon alms, upreared,
From man, from God, from nature, till the soul
At that so huge indulgence stands amazed.
Leave not, my soul, the unfoughten field, nor leave
Thy debts dishonoured, nor thy place desert
Without due service rendered. For thy life,
Up, spirit, and defend that fort of clay,
Thy body, now beleaguered; whether soon
Or late she fall; whether to-day thy friends

Bewail thee dead, or, after years, a man
Grown old in honour and the friend of peace.
Contend, my soul, for moments and for hours;
Each is with service pregnant; each reclaimed
Is as a kingdom conquered, where to reign.
As when a captain rallies to the fight
His scattered legions, and beats ruin back,
He, on the field, encamps, well pleased in mind.
Yet surely him shall fortune overtake,
Him smite in turn, headlong his ensigns drive;
And that dear land, now safe, tomorrow fall.
But he, unthinking, in the present good
Solely delights, and all the camps rejoice.

It is not yours, O mother, to complain,
Not, mother, yours to weep,
Though nevermore your son again
Shall to your bosom creep,
Though nevermore again you watch your baby sleep.

Though in the greener paths of earth,
Mother and child, no more
We wander; and no more the birth
Of me whom once you bore
Seems still the brave reward that once it seemed of yore;
Though as all passes, day and night,
The seasons and the years,
From you, O mother, this delight,
This also disappears —
Some profit yet survives of all your pangs and tears.
The child, the seed, the grain of corn,
The acorn on the hill,
Each for some separate end is born
In season fit, and still
Each must in strength arise to work the almighty will.
So from the hearth the children flee,
By that almighty hand
Austerely led; so one by sea
Goes forth, and one by land;
Nor aught of all man's sons escapes from that command.
So from the sally each obeys
The unseen almighty nod;
So till the ending all their ways
Blindfolded loth have trod:
Nor knew their task at all, but were the tools of God.
And as the fervent smith of yore
Beat out the glowing blade,
Nor wielded in the front of war
The weapons that he made,
But in the tower at home still plied his ringing trade;

So like a sword the son shall roam
On nobler missions sent;
And as the smith remained at home

In peaceful turret pent,
So sits the while at home the mother well content.

THE SICK CHILD

CHILD
O Mother, lay your hand on my brow!
O mother, mother, where am I now?
Why is the room so gaunt and great?
Why am I lying awake so late?

MOTHER
Fear not at all: the night is still.
Nothing is here that means you ill —
Nothing but lamps the whole town through,
And never a child awake but you.

CHILD
Mother, mother, speak low in my ear,
Some of the things are so great and near,
Some are so small and far away,
I have a fear that I cannot say.
What have I done, and what do I fear,
And why are you crying, mother dear?

MOTHER
Out in the city, sounds begin,
Thank the kind God, the carts come in!
An hour or two more, and God is so kind,
The day shall be blue in the window-blind,
Then shall my child go sweetly asleep,
And dream of the birds and the hills of sheep.

IN MEMORIAM F.A.S.

Yet, O stricken heart, remember, O remember
How of human days he lived the better part.
April came to bloom and never dim December
Breathed its killing chills upon the head or heart.
Doomed to know not Winter, only Spring, a being
Trod the flowery April blithely for a while,
Took his fill of music, joy of thought and seeing,
Came and stayed and went, nor ever ceased to smile.
Came and stayed and went, and now when all is finished,
You alone have crossed the melancholy stream,
Yours the pang, but his, O his, the undiminished
Undecaying gladness, undeparted dream.
All that life contains of torture, toil, and treason,
Shame, dishonour, death, to him were but a name.
Here, a boy, he dwelt through all the singing season,
And ere the day of sorrow departed as he came.
Davos.

TO MY FATHER

Peace and her huge invasion to these shores
Puts daily home; innumerable sails
Dawn on the far horizon and draw near;
Innumerable loves, uncounted hopes
To our wild coasts, not darkling now, approach:

Not now obscure, since thou and thine are there,
And bright on the lone isle, the foundered reef,
The long, resounding foreland, Pharos stands.
These are thy works, O father, these thy crown;
Whether on high the air be pure, they shine
Along the yellowing sunset, and all night
Among the unnumbered stars of God they shine;
Or whether fogs arise and far and wide
The low sea-level drown — each finds a tongue
And all night long the tolling bell resounds:
So shine, so toll, till night be overpast,
Till the stars vanish, till the sun return,
And in the haven rides the fleet secure.
In the first hour, the seaman in his skiff
Moves through the unmoving bay, to where the town
Its earliest smoke into the air upbreathes,
And the rough hazels climb along the beach.
To the tugged oar the distant echo speaks.
The ship lies resting, where by reef and roost
Thou and thy lights have led her like a child.
This hast thou done, and I — can I be base?
I must arise, O father, and to port
Some lost, complaining seaman pilot home.

IN THE STATES

With half a heart I wander here
As from an age gone by
A brother — yet though young in years,
An elder brother, I.

You speak another tongue than mine,
Though both were English born.
I towards the night of time decline
You mount into the morn.
Youth shall grow great and strong and free,
But age must still decay:
Tomorrow for the States, — for me,
England and Yesterday.
San Francisco.

A PORTRAIT

I am a kind of farthing dip,
Unfriendly to the nose and eyes;
A blue-behinded ape, I skip
Upon the trees of Paradise.
At mankind's feast, I take my place
In solemn, sanctimonious state,
And have the air of saying grace
While I defile the dinner-plate.
I am "the smiler with the knife,"
The battener upon garbage, I —
Dear Heaven, with such a rancid life
Were it not better far to die?
Yet still, about the human pale,
I love to scamper, love to race,
To swing by my irreverent tail
All over the most holy place;

And when at length, some golden day,
The unfailing sportsman, aiming at,
Shall bag, me — all the world shall say:
Thank God, and there's an end of that!

Sing clearlier, Muse, or evermore be still,
Sing truer or no longer sing!
No more the voice of melancholy Jaques
To wake a weeping echo in the hill;
But as the boy, the pirate of the spring,
From the green elm a living linnet takes,
One natural verse recapture — then be still.

A CAMP

The bed was made, the room was fit,
By punctual eve the stars were lit;
The air was still, the water ran,
No need was there for maid or man,
When we put up, my ass and I,
At God's green caravanserai.

THE COUNTRY OF THE CAMISARDS

We travelled in the print of olden wars;
Yet all the land was green;
And love we found, and peace,
Where fire and war had been.

They pass and smile, the children of the sword —
No more the sword they wield;
And O, how deep the corn
Along the battlefield!

SKERRYVORE

For love of lovely words, and for the sake
Of those, my kinsmen and my countrymen,
Who early and late in the windy ocean toiled
To plant a star for seamen, where was then
The surfy haunt of seals and cormorants:
I, on the lintel of this cot, inscribe
The name of a strong tower.

SKERRYVORE
THE PARALLEL

Here all is sunny, and when the truant gull
Skims the green level of the lawn, his wing
Dispetals roses; here the house is framed
Of kneaded brick and the plumed mountain pine,
Such clay as artists fashion and such wood
As the tree-climbing urchin breaks. But there
Eternal granite hewn from the living isle
And dowelled with brute iron, rears a tower
That from its wet foundation to its crown
Of glittering glass, stands, in the sweep of winds,
Immovable, immortal, eminent.

My house, I say. But hark to the sunny doves
That make my roof the arena of their loves,
That gyre about the gable all day long
And fill the chimneys with their murmurous song:
Our house, they say; and *mine*, the cat declares
And spreads his golden fleece upon the chairs;
And *mine* the dog, and rises stiff with wrath
If any alien foot profane the path.
So too the buck that trimmed my terraces,
Our whilome gardener, called the garden his;
Who now, deposed, surveys my plain abode
And his late kingdom, only from the road.

My body which my dungeon is,
And yet my parks and palaces: —
Which is so great that there I go
All the day long to and fro,
And when the night begins to fall
Throw down my bed and sleep, while all
The building hums with wakefulness —
Even as a child of savages
When evening takes her on her way
(She having roamed a summer's day
Along the mountainsides and scalp),
Sleeps in an antre of that alp: —
Which is so broad and high that there,
As in the topless fields of air,
My fancy soars like to a kite
And faints in the blue infinite: —
Which is so strong, my strongest throes
And the rough world's besieging blows

Not break it, and so weak withal,
Death ebbs and flows in its loose wall
As the green sea in fishers' nets,
And tops its topmost parapets: —
Which is so wholly mine that I
Can wield its whole artillery,
And mine so little, that my soul

Dwells in perpetual control,
And I but think and speak and do
As my dead fathers move me to: —
If this born body of my bones
The beggared soul so barely owns,
What money passed from hand to hand,
What creeping custom of the land,
What deed of author or assign,
Can make a house a thing of mine?

Say not of me that weakly I declined
The labours of my sires, and fled the sea,
The towers we founded and the lamps we lit,
To play at home with paper like a child.
But rather say: *In the afternoon of time*
A strenuous family dusted from its hands
The sand of granite, and beholding far
Along the sounding coast its pyramids
And tall memorials catch the dying sun,
Smiled well content, and to this childish task
Around the fire addressed its evening hours.

BOOK II

IN SCOTS

TABLE OF COMMON SCOTTISH VOWEL SOUNDS

ae

ai } = open A *as in* rare.

a'

au

aw } = AW *as in* law.

ea = open E *as in* mere, but this with exceptions, as heather = heather, wean = wain, lear = lair.

ee

ei

ie } = open E *as in* mere.

oa = open O *as in* more.

ou = doubled O *as in* poor.

ow = OW *as in* bower.

u = doubled O *as in* poor.

ui *or* ü before R = (say roughly) open A *as in* rare.

ui *or* ü before any other consonant = (say roughly) close I *as in* grin.

y = open I *as in* kite.

i = pretty nearly what you please, much as in English, Heaven guide the reader through that labyrinth! But in Scots it dodges usually from the short I, *as in* grin, to the open E *as in* mere. Find and blind, I may remark, are pronounced to rhyme with the preterite of grin.

THE MAKER TO POSTERITY

Far 'yont amang the years to be,
When a' we think, an' a' we see,
An' a' we luve, 's been dung ajee
   By time's rouch shouther,
An' what was richt and wrang for me
   Lies mangled throu'ther,
It's possible — it's hardly mair —
That some ane, ripin' after lear —
Some auld professor or young heir,
   If still there's either —
May find an' read me, an' be sair
   Perplexed, puir brither!

"What tongue does your auld bookie speak?"
He'll speir; an' I, his mou' to steik:
"No' bein' fit to write in Greek,
   I wrote in Lallan,
Dear to my heart as the peat-reek,
   Auld as Tantallon.

"Few spak it than, an' noo there's nane.
My puir auld sangs lie a' their lane,
Their sense, that aince was braw an' plain,
   Tint a'thegither,
Like runes upon a standin' stane
   Amang the heather.

"But think not you the brae to speel;
You, tae, maun chow the bitter peel;
For a' your lear, for a' your skeel,
   Ye're nane sae lucky;
An' things are mebbe waur than weel
   For you, my buckie.

"The hale concern (baith hens an' eggs,
Baith books an' writers, stars an' clegs)
Noo stachers upon lowsent legs
   An' wears awa';
The tack o' mankind, near the dregs,
   Rins unco law.

"Your book, that in some braw new tongue
Ye wrote or prentit, preached or sung,
Will still be just a bairn, an' young
   In fame an' years,
Whan the hale planet's guts are dung
   About your ears;

"An' you, sair gruppin' to a spar
Or whammled wi' some bleezin' star,
Cryin' to ken whaur deil ye are,
   Hame, France, or Flanders —
Whang sindry like a railway car
   An' flie in danders."

ILLE TERRARUM

Frae nirly, nippin', Eas'lan' breeze,
Frae Norlan' snaw, an' haar o' seas,
Weel happit in your gairden trees,
A bonny bit,
Atween the muckle Pentland's knees,
Secure ye sit.

Beeches an' aiks entwine their theek,
An' firs, a stench, auld-farrant clique.
A simmer day, your chimleys reek,
Couthy and bien;
An' here an' there your windies keek
Amang the green.
A pickle plats an' paths an' posies,
A wheen auld gillyflowers an' roses:
A ring o' wa's the hale encloses
Frae sheep or men:
An' there the auld housie beeks an' dozes,
A' by her lane.
The gairdner crooks his weary back
A' day in the pitaty-track,
Or mebbe stops a while to crack
Wi' Jane the cook,
Or at some buss, worm-eaten-black,
To gie a look.
Frae the high hills the curlew ca's;
The sheep gang baaing by the wa's;
Or whiles a clan o' roosty craws
Cangle thegither;
The wild bees seek the gairden raws,
Weariet wi' heather.
Or in the gloamin' douce an' grey
The sweet-throat mavis tunes her lay;
The herd comes linkin' doun the brae;
An' by degrees
The muckle siller müne maks way
Amang the trees.

Here aft hae I, wi' sober heart,
For meditation sat apairt,
When orra loves or kittle art
Perplexed my mind;
Here socht a balm for ilka smart
O' humankind.
Here aft, weel neukit by my lane,
Wi' Horace, or perhaps Montaigne,
The mornin' hours hae come an' gane
Abüne my heid —
I wadna gi'en a chucky-stane
For a' I'd read.
But noo the auld city, street by street,
An' winter fu' o' snaw an' sleet,

A while shut in my gangrel feet
An' goavin' mettle;
Noo is the soopit ingle sweet,
An' liltin' kettle.
An' noo the winter winds complain;
Cauld lies the glaur in ilka lane;
On draigled hizzie, tautit wean
An' drucken lads,
In the mirk nicht, the winter rain
Dribbles an' blads.
Whan bugles frae the Castle rock,
An' beaten drums wi' dowie shock,
Wauken, at cauld-rife sax o'clock,
My chitterin' frame,
I mind me on the kintry cock,
The kintry hame.

I mind me on yon bonny bield;
An' Fancy traivels far afield
To gaither a' that gairdens yield
O' sun an' Simmer:
To hearten up a dowie chield,
Fancy's the limmer!

When aince Aprile has fairly come,
An' birds may bigg in winter's lum,
An' pleesure's spreid for a' and some
O' whatna state,
Love, wi' her auld recruitin' drum,
Than taks the gate.
The heart plays dunt wi' main an' micht;
The lasses' een are a' sae bricht,
Their dresses are sae braw an' ticht,
The bonny birdies! —
Puir winter virtue at the sicht
Gangs heels ower hurdies.
An' aye as love frae land to land
Tirls the drum wi' eident hand,
A' men collect at her command,
Toun-bred or land'art,
An' follow in a denty band
Her gaucy standart.
An' I, wha sang o' rain an' snaw,
An' weary winter weel awa',
Noo busk me in a jacket braw,
An' tak my place
I' the ram-stam, harum-scarum raw,
Wi' smilin' face.

A MILE AN' A BITTOCK

A mile an' a bittock, a mile or twa,
Abüne the burn, ayont the law,
Davie an' Donal' an' Cherlie an' a',
An' the müne was shinin' clearly!
Ane went hame wi' the ither, an' then
The ither went hame wi' the ither twa men,
An' baith wad return him the service again,
An' the müne was shinin' clearly!
The clocks were chappin' in house an' ha',
Eleeven, twal an' ane an' twa;
An' the guidman's face was turnt to the wa'
An' the müne was shinin' clearly!
A wind got up frae affa the sea,
It blew the stars as clear's could be,
It blew in the een of a' o' the three,
An' the müne was shinin' clearly!
Noo, Davie was first to get sleep in his head,
"The best o' frien's maun twine," he said;
"I'm weariet, an' here I'm awa' to my bed."
An' the müne was shinin' clearly!
Twa o' them walkin' an' crackin' their lane,
The mornin' licht cam grey an' plain,
An' the birds they yammert on stick an' stane,
An' the müne was shinin' clearly!
O years ayont, O years awa',
My lads, ye'll mind whate'er befa' —
My lads, ye'll mind on the bield o' the law,
When the müne was shinin' clearly.

A LOWDEN SABBATH MORN

The clinkum-clank o' Sabbath bells
Noo to the hoastin' rookery swells,
Noo faintin' laigh in shady dells,
Sounds far an' near,
An' through the simmer kintry tells
Its tale o' cheer.

An' noo, to that melodious play,
A' deidly awn the quiet sway —
A' ken their solemn holiday,
Bestial an' human,
The singin' lintie on the brae,
The restin' plou'man.

He, mair than a' the lave o' men,
His week completit joys to ken;
Half-dressed, he daunders out an' in,
Perplext wi' leisure;
An' his raxt limbs he'll rax again
Wi' painfü' pleesure.

The steerin' mither strang afit
Noo shoos the bairnies but a bit;
Noo cries them ben, their Sinday shüit
To scart upon them,
Or sweeties in their pooch to pit,
Wi' blessin's on them.

The lasses, clean frae tap to taes,
Are busked in crunklin' underclaes;
The gartened hose, the weel-fllled stays,
The nakit shift,
A' bleached on bonny greens for days,
An' white's the drift.

An' noo to face the kirkward mile:
The guidman's hat o' dacent style,
The blackit shoon we noo maun fyle
As white's the miller:
A waefü' peety tae, to spile
The warth o' siller.

Our Marg'et, aye sae keen to crack,
Douce-stappin' in the stoury track,
Her emerald goun a' kiltit back
Frae snawy coats,
White-ankled, leads the kirkward pack
Wi' Dauvit Groats.

A thocht ahint, in runkled breeks,
A' spiled wi' lyin' by for weeks,
The guidman follows closs, an' cleiks
The sonsie missis;
His sarious face at aince bespeaks
The day that this is.

And aye an' while we nearer draw
To whaur the kirkton lies alaw,

Mair neebours, comin' saft an' slaw
Frae here an' there,
The thicker thrang the gate an' caw
The stour in air.
But hark! the bells frae nearer clang;
To rowst the slaw their sides they bang;
An' see! black coats a'ready thrang
The green kirkyaird;
And at the yett, the chestnuts spang
That brocht the laird.

The solemn elders at the plate
Stand drinkin' deep the pride o' state:
The practised hands as gash an' great
As Lords o' Session;
The later named, a wee thing blate
In their expression.
The prentit stanes that mark the deid,
Wi' lengthened lip, the sarious read;
Syne wag a moraleesin' heid,
An' then an' there
Their hirplin' practice an' their creed
Try hard to square.
It's here our Merren lang has lain,
A wee bewast the table-stane;
An' yon's the grave o' Sandy Blane;
An' further ower,
The mither's brithers, dacent men!
Lie a' the fower.
Here the guidman sall bide awee
To dwall amang the deid; to see
Auld faces clear in fancy's e'e;
Belike to hear
Auld voices fa'in' saft an' slee
On fancy's ear.
Thus, on the day o' solemn things,
The bell that in the steeple swings
To fauld a scaittered faim'ly rings
Its walcome screed;
An' just a wee thing nearer brings
The quick an' deid.

But noo the bell is ringin' in;
To tak their places, folk begin;
The minister himsel' will shüne
Be up the gate,
Filled fu' wi' clavers about sin
An' man's estate.
The tünes are up — *French*, to be shüre,
The faithfü' *French*, an' twa-three mair;
The auld prezentor, hoastin' sair,
Wales out the portions,
An' yirks the tüne into the air
Wi' queer contortions.

Follows the prayer, the readin' next,
An' than the fisslin' for the text —
The twa-three last to find it, vext
But kind o' proud;
An' than the peppermints are raxed,
An' southernwood.
For noo's the time whan pows are seen
Nid-noddin' like a mandareen;
When tenty mithers stap a preen
In sleepin' weans;
An' nearly half the parochine
Forget their pains.
There's just a waukrif twa or three:
Thrawn commentautors sweer to 'gree,
Weans glowrin' at the bumlin' bee
On windie-glasses,
Or lads that tak a keek a-glee
At sonsie lasses.

Himsel', meanwhile, frae whaur he cocks
An' bobs belaw the soundin'-box,
The treasures of his words unlocks
Wi' prodigality,
An' deals some unco dingin' knocks
To infidality.
Wi' sappy unction, hoo he burkes
The hopes o' men that trust in works,
Expounds the fau'ts o' ither kirks,
An' shaws the best o' them
No' muckle better than mere Turks,
When a's confessed o' them.
Bethankit! what a bonny creed!
What mair would ony Christian need? —
The braw words rummle ower his heid,
Nor steer the sleeper;
An' in their restin' graves, the deid
Sleep aye the deeper.

Note. — It may be guessed by some that I had a certain parish in my eye, and this makes it proper I should add a word of disclamation. In my time there have been two ministers in that parish. Of the first I have a special reason to speak well, even had there been any to think ill. The second I have often met in private and long (in the due phrase) "sat under" in his church, and neither here nor there have I heard an unkind or ugly word upon his lips. The preacher of the text had thus no original in that particular parish; but when I was a boy, he might have been observed in many others; he was then (like the schoolmaster) abroad; and by recent advices, it would seem he has not yet entirely disappeared. — [R. L. S.]

THE SPAEWIFE

O, I wad like to ken — to the beggar-wife says I —
Why chops are guid to brander and nane sae guid to fry.
An' siller, that's sae braw to keep, is brawer still to gi'e.
— *It's gey an' easy speirin'*, says the beggar-wife to me.
O, I wad like to ken — to the beggar-wife says I —
Hoo a' things come to be whaur we find them when we try.
The lassies in their claes an' the fishes in the sea.
— *It's gey an' easy speirin'*, says the beggar-wife to me.
O' I wad like to ken — to the beggar-wife says I —
Why lads are a' to sell an' lasses a' to buy;
An' naebody for dacency but barely twa or three.
— *It's gey an' easy speirin'*, says the beggar-wife to me.
O, I wad like to ken — to the beggar-wife says I —
Gin death's as shüre to men as killin' is to kye,
Why God has filled the yearth sae fu' o' tasty things to pree.
— *It's gey an' easy speirin'*, says the beggar-wife to me.
O, I wad like to ken — to the beggar-wife says I —
The reason o' the cause an' the wherefore o' the why,
Wi' mony anither riddle brings the tear into my e'e.
— *It's gey an' easy speirin'*, says the beggar-wife to me.

THE BLAST —

It's rainin'. Weet's the gairden sod,
Weet the lang roads whaur gangrels plod —
A maist unceevil thing o' God
In mid July —
If ye'll just curse the sneckdraw, dod!
An' sae wull I!

He's a braw place in Heev'n, ye ken,
An' lea's us puir, forjaskit men
Clamjamfried in the but and ben
He ca's the earth —
A wee bit inconvenient den
No muckle worth;
An' whiles, at orra times, keeks out,
Sees what puir mankind are about;
An' if He can, I've little doubt,
Upsets their plans;
He hates a' mankind, brainch and root,
An' a' that's man's.
An' whiles, whan they tak' heart again,
An' life i' the sun looks braw an' plain,
Doun comes a jaw o' droukin' rain
Upon their honours —
God sends a spate out ower the plain,
Or mebbe thun'ers.
Lord safe us, life's an unco thing!
Simmer and Winter, Yule an' Spring,
The damned, dour-heartit seasons bring
A feck o' trouble.
I wadna try 't to be a king —
No, nor for double.
But since we're in it, willy-nilly,
We maun be watchfü', wise an' skilly,
An' no' mind ony ither billy,
Lassie nor God.
But drink — that's my best counsel till 'e;
Sae tak' the nod.

THE COUNTERBLAST —

My bonny man, the warld, it's true,
Was made for neither me nor you;
It's just a place to warstle through,
As Job confessed o't;
And aye the best that we'll can do
Is mak' the best o't.
There's rowth o' wrang, I'm free to say:
The simmer brunt, the winter blae,
The face of earth a' fyled wi' clay
An' dour wi' chuckies,
An' life a rough an' land'art play
For country buckies.
An' food's anither name for clart;
An' beasts an' brambles bite an' scart;
An' what would WE be like, my heart!
If bared o' claethin'?
— Aweel, I canna mend your cart:
It's that or naethin'.
A feck o' folk frae first to last
Have through this queer experience passed;
Twa-three, I ken, just damn an' blast
The hale transaction;
But twa-three ithers, east an' wast,
Fand satisfaction.
Whaur braid the briery muirs expand,
A waefü' an' a weary land,
The bumble-bees, a gowden band,
Are blithely hingin';
An' there the canty wanderer fand
The laverock singin'.

Trout in the burn grow great as herr'n';
The simple sheep can find their fair'n';
The winds blaws clean about the cairn
Wi' caller air;
The muircock an' the barefit bairn
Are happy there.
Sic-like the howes o' life to some:
Green loans whaur they ne'er fash their thumb,
But mark the muckle winds that come,
Soopin' an' cool,
Or hear the powrin' burnie drum
In the shilfa's pool.
The evil wi' the guid they tak';
They ca' a grey thing grey, no' black;
To a steigh brae a stubborn back
Addressin' daily;
An' up the rude, unbieldy track
O' life, gang gaily.
What you would like's a palace ha',
Or Sinday parlour dink an' braw

Wi' a' things ordered in a raw
By denty leddies.
Weel, then, ye canna hae't: that's a'
That to be said is.
An' since at life ye've ta'en the grue,
An' winna blithely hirsle through,
Ye've fund the very thing to do —
That's to drink speerit;
An' shüne we'll hear the last o' you —
An' blithe to hear it!

The shoon ye coft, the life ye lead,
Ithers will heir when aince ye're deid;
They'll heir your tasteless bite o' breid,
An' find it sappy;
They'll to your dulefü' house succeed,
An' there be happy.
As whan a glum an' fractious wean
Has sat an' sullened by his lane
Till, wi' a rowstin' skelp, he's ta'en
An' shoo'd to bed — —
The ither bairns a' fa' to play'n',
As gleg's a gled.

THE COUNTERBLAST IRONICAL

It's strange that God should fash to frame
The yearth and lift sae hie,
An' clean forget to explain the same
To a gentleman like me.
Thae gusty, donnered ither folk,
Their weird they weel may dree;
But why present a pig in a poke
To a gentleman like me?
Thae ither folk their parritch eat
An' sup their sugared tea;
But the mind is no' to be wyled wi' meat
Wi' a gentleman like me.
Thae ither folk, they court their joes
At gloamin' on the lea;
But they're made of a commoner clay, I suppose,
Than a gentleman like me.

Thae ither folk, for richt or wrang,
They suffer, bleed, or dee;
But a' thir things are an emp'y sang
To a gentleman like me.
It's a different thing that I demand,
Tho' humble as can be —
A statement fair in my Maker's hand
To a gentleman like me:
A clear account writ fair an' broad,
An' a plain apologie;
Or the deevil a ceevil word to God
From a gentleman like me.

THEIR LAUREATE TO AN ACADEMY CLASS

DINNER CLUB

Dear Thamson class, whaure'er I gang
It aye comes ower me wi' a spang:
*"Lordsake! thae Thamson lads — (deil hang
Or else Lord mend them!) —
An' that wanchancy annual sang
I ne'er can send them!"*
Straucht, at the name, a trusty tyke,
My conscience girrs ahint the dyke;
Straucht on my hinderlands I fyke
To find a rhyme t' ye;
Pleased — although mebbe no' pleased-like —
To gie my time t' ye.

"Weel," an' says you, wi' heavin' breist,
*"Sae far, sae guid, but what's the neist?
Yearly we gather to the feast,
A' hopefu' men —
Yearly we skelloch 'Hang the beast —
Nae sang again!'"*
My lads, an' what am I to say?
Ye shürely ken the Muse's way:
Yestreen, as gleg's a tyke — the day,
Thrawn like a cuddy:
Her conduc', that to her's a play,
Deith to a body.
Aft whan I sat an' made my mane,
Aft whan I laboured burd-alane
Fishin' for rhymes an' findin' nane,
Or nane were fit for ye —
Ye judged me cauld's a chucky-stane —
No car'n' a bit for ye!

But saw ye ne'er some pingein' bairn
As weak as a pitaty-par'n' —
Less üsed wi' guidin' horseshoe aim
Than steerin' crowdie —
Packed aff his lane, by moss an' cairn,
To ca' the howdie.
Wae's me, for the puir callant than!
He wambles like a poke o' bran,
An' the lowse rein, as hard's he can,
Pu's, trem'lin' handit;
Till, blaff! upon his hinderlan'
Behauld him landit.

Sic-like — I awn the weary fac' —
Whan on my muse the gate I tak',
An' see her gleed e'e raxin' back
To keek ahint her; —
To me, the brig o' Heev'n gangs black
As blackest winter.
"Lordsake! we're aff," thinks I, *"but whaur?*

*On what abhorred an' whinny scaur,
Or whammled in what sea o' glaur,
Will she desert me?
An' will she just disgrace? or waur —
Will she no' hurt me?"*
Kittle the quære! But at least
The day I've backed the fashious beast,
While she, wi' mony a spang an' reist,
 Flang heels ower bonnet;
An' a' triumphant — for your feast,
 Hae! there's your sonnet!

EMBRO HIE KIRK

The Lord Himsel' in former days
Waled out the proper tunes for praise
An' named the proper kind o' claes
For folk to preach in:
Preceese and in the chief o' ways
Important teachin'.
He ordered a' things late and air';
He ordered folk to stand at prayer
(Although I canna just mind where
He gave the warnin'),
An' pit pomatum on their hair
On Sabbath mornin'.

The hale o' life by His commands
Was ordered to a body's hands;
But see! this *corpus juris* stands
By a' forgotten;
An' God's religion in a' lands
Is deid an' rotten.
While thus the lave o' mankind's lost,
O' Scotland still God maks His boast —
Puir Scotland, on whase barren coast
A score or twa
Auld wives wi' mutches an' a hoast
Still keep His law.
In Scotland, a wheen canty, plain,
Douce, kintry-leevin' folk retain
The Truth — or did so aince — alane
Of a' men leevin';
An' noo just twa o' them remain —
Just Begg an' Niven.
For noo, unfaithfü' to the Lord,
Auld Scotland joins the rebel horde;
Her human hymn-books on the board
She noo displays:
An' Embro Hie Kirk's been restored
In popish ways.
O *punctum temporis* for action
To a' o' the reformin' faction,
If yet, by ony act or paction,
Thocht, word, or sermon,
This dark an' damnable transaction
Micht yet determine!

For see — as Doctor Begg explains —
Hoo easy 't's düne! a pickle weans,
Wha in the Hie Street gaither stanes
By his instruction,
The uncovenantit, pentit panes
Ding to destruction.
Up, Niven, or ower late — an' dash
Laigh in the glaur that carnal hash;

Let spires and pews wi' gran' stramash
Thegither fa';
The rumlin' kist o' whustles smash
In pieces sma'.
Noo choose ye out a walie hammer;
About the knottit buttress clam'er;
Alang the steep roof stoyt an' stammer,
A gate mischancy;
On the aul' spire, the bells' hie cha'mer,
Dance your bit dancie.
Ding, devel, dunt, destroy, an' ruin,
Wi' carnal stanes the square bestrewn',
Till your loud chaps frae Kyle to Fruin,
Frae Hell to Heeven,
Tell the guid wark that baith are doin' —
Baith Begg an' Niven.

THE SCOTSMAN'S RETURN FROM ABROAD

IN A LETTER FROM MR. THOMSON TO MR. JOHNSTONE

In mony a foreign pairt I've been,
An' mony an unco ferlie seen,
Since, Mr. Johnstone, you and I,
Last walkit upon Cocklerye.

Wi' gleg, observant een, I pass't
By sea an' land, through East an' Wast,
And still in ilka age an' station
Saw naething but abomination.
In thir uncovenantit lands
The gangrel Scot uplifts his hands
At lack of a' sectarian füsh'n,
An' cauld religious destitütion.
He rins, puir man, frae place to place,
Tries a' their graceless means o' grace,
Preacher on preacher, kirk on kirk —
This yin a stot an' thon a stirk —
A bletherin' clan, no warth a preen.
As bad as Smith of Aiberdeen!

At last, across the weary faem,
Frae far, outlandish pairts I came.
On ilka side o' me I fand
Fresh tokens o' my native land.
Wi' whatna joy I hailed them a' —
The hill-taps standin' raw by raw,
The public-house, the Hielan' birks,
And a' the bonny U.P. kirks!
But maistly thee, the bluid o' Scots,
Frae Maidenkirk to John o' Groats!
The king o' drinks, as I conceive it,
Talisker, Isla, or Glenlivet!

For after years wi' a pockmantie
Frae Zanzibar to Alicante,
In mony a fash and sair affliction
I gie't as my sincere conviction —
Of a' their foreign tricks an' pliskies,
I maist aborninate their whiskies.
Nae doot, themsel's, they ken it weel,
An' wi' a hash o' leemon peel,

And ice an' siccan filth, they ettle
The stawsome kind o' goo to settle
Sic wersh apothecary's broos wi'
As Scotsmen scorn to fyle their moo's wi'.
An', man, I was a blithe hame-comer
Whan first I syndit out my rummer.
Ye should hae seen me then, wi' care
The less important pairts prepare;
Syne, weel contentit wi' it a',
Pour in the speerits wi' a jaw!
I didna drink, I didna speak, —

I only snowkit up the reek.
I was sae pleased therein to paidle,
I sat an' plowtered wi' my ladle.
An' blithe was I, the morrow's morn,
To daunder through the stookit corn,
And after a' my strange mishanters
Sit doun amang my ain dissenters
An', man, it was a joy to me
The pu'pit an' the pews to see,
The pennies dirlin' in the plate,
The elders lookin' on in state;
An' 'mang the first, as it befell,
Wha should I see, sir, but yoursel'!
I was, and I will no' deny it,
At the first gliff a hantle tryit
To see yoursel' in sic a station —
It seemed a doubtfü' dispensation.
The feelin' was a mere digression;
For shüne I understood the session,
An' mindin' Aiken an' M'Neil,
I wondered they had düne sae weel.
I saw I had mysel' to blame;
For had I but remained at hame,

Aiblins — though no ava' deservin' 't —
They micht hae named your humble servant.
The kirk was filled, the door was steiked;
Up to the pu'pit aince I keeked;
I was mair pleased than I can tell —
It was the minister himsel'!
Proud, proud was I to see his face,
After sae lang awa' frae grace.
Pleased as I was, I'm no' denyin'
Some maitters were not edifyin';
For first I fand — an' here was news! —
Mere hymn-books cockin' in the pews —
A humanised abomination,
Unfit for ony congregation.
Syne, while I still was on the tenter,
I scunnered at the new prezentor;
I thocht him gesterin' an' cauld —
A sair declension frae the auld.
Syne, as though a' the faith was wreckit,
The prayer was not what I'd exspeckit.
Himsel', as it appeared to me,
Was no' the man he üsed to be.
But just as I was growin' vext
He waled a maist judeecious text,
An', launchin' into his prelections,
Swoopt, wi' a skirl, on a' defections.
O what a gale was on my speerit
To hear the p'ints o' doctrine clearit,
And a' the horrors o' damnation

Set furth wi' faithfü' ministration!
Nae shauchlin' testimony here —
We were a' damned, an' that was clear.
I owned, wi' gratitude an' wonder,
He was a pleesure to sit under.

Late in the nicht in bed I lay,
The winds were at their weary play,
An' tirlin' wa's an' skirlin' wae
Through Heev'n they battered; —
On-ding o' hail, on-blaff o' spray,
The tempest blattered.
The masoned house it dinled through;
It dung the ship, it cowped the coo;
The rankit aiks it overthrew,
Had braved a' weathers;
The strang sea-gleds it took an' blew
Awa' like feethers.
The thrawes o' fear on a' were shed,
An' the hair rose, an' slumber fled,
An' lichts were lit an' prayers were said
Through a' the kintry;
An' the cauld terror clum in bed
Wi' a' an' sindry.
To hear in the pit-mirk on hie
The brangled collieshangie flie,
The warl', they thocht, wi' land an' sea,
Itsel' wad cowpit;
An' for auld airn, the smashed débris
By God be rowpit.
Meanwhile frae far Aldeboran
To folks wi' talescopes in han',
O' ships that cowpit, winds that ran,
Nae sign was seen,
But the wee warl' in sunshine span
As bricht's a preen.

I, tae, by God's especial grace,
Dwall denty in a bieldy place,
Wi' hosened feet, wi' shaven face,
Wi' dacent mainners:
A grand example to the race
O' tautit sinners!
The wind may blaw, the heathen rage,
The deil may start on the rampage; —
The sick in bed, the thief in cage —
What's a' to me?
Cosh in my house, a sober sage,
I sit an' see.
An' whiles the bluid spangs to my bree,
To lie sae saft, to live sae free,
While better men maun do an' die
In unco places.
"*Whaur's God?*" I cry, an' "*Whae is me*

To hae sic graces?"
I mind the fecht the sailors keep,
But fire or can'le, rest or sleep,
In darkness an' the muckle deep;
An' mind beside
The herd that on the hills o' sheep
Has wandered wide.
I mind me on the hoastin' weans —
The penny joes on causey-stanes —
The auld folk wi' the crazy banes,
Baith auld an' puir,
That aye maun thole the winds an' rains
An' labour sair.

An' whiles I'm kind o' pleased a blink,
An' kind o' fleyed forby, to think,
For a' my rowth o' meat an' drink
An' waste o' crumb,
I'll mebbe have to thole wi' skink
In Kingdom Come.
For God whan jowes the Judgment bell
Wi' His ain Hand, His Leevin' Sel',
Sall ryve the guid (as Prophets tell)
Frae them that had it;
And in the reamin' pat o' Hell,
The rich be scaddit.
O Lord, if this indeed be sae,
Let daw' that sair an' happy day!
Again the warl', grawn auld an' grey,
Up wi' your aixe!
An' let the puir enjoy their play —
I'll thole my paiks.

MY CONSCIENCE!

Of a' the ills that flesh can fear,
The loss o' frien's, the lack o' gear,
A yowlin' tyke, a glandered mear,
A lassie's nonsense —
There's just ae thing I canna bear,
An' that's my conscience.

Whan day (an' a' excüse) has gane,
An' wark is düne, and duty's plain,
An' to my chalmer a' my lane
I creep apairt,
My conscience! hoo the yammerin' pain
Stends to my heart!

A' day wi' various ends in view,
The hairsts o' time I had to pu',
An' made a hash wad staw a soo,
Let be a man! —
My conscience! whan my han's were fu',
Whaur were ye than?

An' there were a' the lures o' life,
There pleasure skirlin' on the fife,
There anger, wi' the hotchin' knife
Ground shairp in Hell —
My conscience! — you that's like a wife! —
Whaur was yoursel'?

I ken it fine: just waitin' here,
To gar the evil waur appear,
To clart the guid, confüse the clear,
Misca' the great,
My conscience! an' to raise a steer
Whan a's ower late.

Sic-like, some tyke grawn auld and blind,
Whan thieves brok' through the gear to p'ind,
Has lain his dozened length an' grinned
At the disaster;
An' the morn's mornin', wud's the wind,
Yokes on his master.

TO DOCTOR JOHN BROWN

Whan the dear doctor, dear to a',
Was still among us here belaw,
I set my pipes his praise to blaw
Wi' a' my speerit;
But noo, dear doctor! he's awa'
An' ne'er can hear it.

By Lyne and Tyne, by Thames and Tees,
By a' the various river Dee's,
In Mars and Manors 'yont the seas
Or here at hame,
Whaure'er there's kindly folk to please,
They ken your name.

They ken your name, they ken your tyke,
They ken the honey from your byke;
But mebbe after a' your fyke,
(The trüth to tell)
It's just your honest Rab they like,
An' no' yoursel'.

As at the gowff, some canny play'r
Should tee a common ba' wi' care —
Should flourish and deleever fair
His souple shintie —
An' the ba' rise into the air,
A leevin' lintie:
Sae in the game we writers play,
There comes to some a bonny day,
When a dear ferlie shall repay
Their years o' strife,
An' like your Rab, their things o' clay
Spreid wings o' life.

Ye scarce deserved it, I'm afraid —
You that had never learned the trade,
But just some idle mornin' strayed
Into the schüle,
An' picked the fiddle up an' played
Like Neil himsel'.

Your e'e was gleg, your fingers dink;
Ye didna fash yoursel' to think,
But wove, as fast as puss can link,
Your denty wab: —
Ye stapped your pen into the ink,
An' there was Rab!

Sinsyne, whaure'er your fortune lay
By dowie den, by canty brae,
Simmer an' winter, nicht an' day,
Rab was aye wi' ye;
An' a' the folk on a' the way
Were blithe to see ye.

O sir, the gods are kind indeed,
An' hauld ye for an honoured heid,

That for a wee bit clarkit screed
Sae weel reward ye,
An' lend — puir Rabbie bein' deid —
His ghaist to guard ye.
For though, whaure'er yoursel' may be,
We've just to turn an' glisk a wee,
An' Rab at heel we're shüre to see
Wi' gladsome caper: —
The bogle of a bogle, he —
A ghaist o' paper!

And as the auld-farrant hero sees
In Hell a bogle Hercules,
Pit there the lesser deid to please,
While he himsel'
Dwalls wi' the muckle gods at ease
Far raised frae Hell:
Sae the true Rabbie far has gane
On kindlier business o' his ain
Wi' aulder frien's; an' his breist-bane
An' stumpie tailie,
He birstles at a new hearth-stane
By James and Ailie.

It's an owercome sooth for age an' youth,
And it brooks wi' nae denial,
That the dearest friends are the auldest friends,
And the young are just on trial.
There's a rival bauld wi' young an' auld,
And it's him that has bereft me;
For the sürest friends are the auldest friends,
And the maist o' mine's hae left me.
There are kind hearts still, for friends to fill
And fools to take and break them;
But the nearest friends are the auldest friends,
And the grave's the place to seek them.

SONGS OF TRAVEL

THE VAGABOND

(TO AN AIR OF SCHUBERT)

Give to me the life I love,
Let the lave go by me,
Give the jolly heaven above
And the byway nigh me.
Bed in the bush with stars to see,
Bread I dip in the river —
There's the life for a man like me,
There's the life for ever.
Let the blow fall soon or late,
Let what will be o'er me;
Give the face of earth around
And the road before me.
Wealth I seek not, hope nor love,
Nor a friend to know me;
All I seek, the heaven above
And the road below me.
Or let autumn fall on me
Where afield I linger,
Silencing the bird on tree,
Biting the blue finger.
White as meal the frosty field —
Warm the fireside haven —
Not to autumn will I yield,
Not to winter even!

Let the blow fall soon or late,
Let what will be o'er me;
Give the face of earth around,
And the road before me.
Wealth I ask not, hope nor love,
Nor a friend to know me.
All I ask, the heaven above
And the road below me.

YOUTH AND LOVE — I

Once only by the garden gate
Our lips were joined and parted.
I must fulfil an empty fate
And travel the uncharted.
Hail and farewell! I must arise,
Leave here the fatted cattle,
And paint on foreign lands and skies
My Odyssey of battle.
The untented Kosmos my abode,
I pass, a wilful stranger:
My mistress still the open road
And the bright eyes of danger.
Come ill or well, the cross, the crown,
The rainbow or the thunder,
I fling my soul and body down
For God to plough them under.

YOUTH AND LOVE — II

To the heart of youth the world is a highwayside.
Passing for ever, he fares; and on either hand,
Deep in the gardens golden pavilions hide,
Nestle in orchard bloom, and far on the level land
Call him with lighted lamp in the eventide.
Thick as the stars at night when the moon is down,
Pleasures assail him. He to his nobler fate
Fares; and but waves a hand as he passes on,
Cries but a wayside word to her at the garden gate,
Sings but a boyish stave and his face is gone.

In dreams, unhappy, I behold you stand
As heretofore:
The unremembered tokens in your hand
Avail no more.
No more the morning glow, no more the grace,
Enshrines, endears.
Cold beats the light of time upon your face
And shows your tears.
He came and went. Perchance you wept a while
And then forgot.
Ah, me! but he that left you with a smile
Forgets you not.

She rested by the Broken Brook,
She drank of Weary Well,
She moved beyond my lingering look,
Ah, whither none can tell!
She came, she went. In other lands,
Perchance in fairer skies,
Her hands shall cling with other hands,
Her eyes to other eyes.
She vanished. In the sounding town,
Will she remember too?
Will she recall the eyes of brown
As I recall the blue?

The infinite shining heavens
Rose and I saw in the night
Uncountable angel stars
Showering sorrow and light.
I saw them distant as heaven,
Dumb and shining and dead,
And the idle stars of the night
Were dearer to me than bread.
Night after night in my sorrow
The stars stood over the sea,
Till lo! I looked in the dusk
And a star had come down to me.

Plain as the glistering planets shine
When winds have cleaned the skies,
Her love appeared, appealed for mine
And wantoned in her eyes.
Clear as the shining tapers burned
On Cytherea's shrine,
Those brimming, lustrous beauties turned,
And called and conquered mine.
The beacon-lamp that Hero lit
No fairer shone on sea,
No plainlier summoned will and wit,
Than hers encouraged me.
I thrilled to feel her influence near,
I struck my flag at sight.
Her starry silence smote my ear
Like sudden drums at night.
I ran as, at the cannon's roar,
The troops the ramparts man —
As in the holy house of yore
The willing Eli ran.
Here, lady, lo! that servant stands
You picked from passing men,
And should you need nor heart nor hands
He bows and goes again.

To you, let snow and roses
And golden locks belong.
These are the world's enslavers,
Let these delight the throng.
For her of duskier lustre
Whose favour still I wear,
The snow be in her kirtle,
The rose be in her hair!
The hue of highland rivers
Careering, full and cool,
From sable on to golden,
From rapid on to pool —
The hue of heather-honey,
The hue of honey-bees,
Shall tinge her golden shoulder,
Shall gild her tawny knees.

Let Beauty awake in the morn from beautiful dreams,
Beauty awake from rest!
Let Beauty awake
For Beauty's sake
In the hour when the birds awake in the brake
And the stars are bright in the west!
Let Beauty awake in the eve from the slumber of day,
Awake in the crimson eve!
In the day's dusk end
When the shades ascend,
Let her wake to the kiss of a tender friend
To render again and receive!

I know not how it is with you —
I love the first and last,
The whole field of the present view,
The whole flow of the past.
One tittle of the things that are,
Nor you should change nor I —
One pebble in our path — one star
In all our heaven of sky.
Our lives, and every day and hour,
One symphony appear:
One road, one garden — every flower
And every bramble dear.

I will make you brooches and toys for your delight
Of bird-song at morning and starshine at night.
I will make a palace fit for you and me
Of green days in forests and blue days at sea.
I will make my kitchen, and you shall keep your room,
Where white flows the river and bright blows the broom,
And you shall wash your linen and keep your body white
In rainfall at morning and dewfall at night.
And this shall be for music when no one else is near,
The fine song for singing, the rare song to hear!
That only I remember, that only you admire,
Of the broad road that stretches and the roadside fire.

WE HAVE LOVED OF YORE

(TO AN AIR OF DIABELLI)

Berried brake and reedy island,
Heaven below, and only heaven above,
Through the sky's inverted azure
Softly swam the boat that bore our love.
Bright were your eyes as the day;
Bright ran the stream,
Bright hung the sky above.
Days of April, airs of Eden,
How the glory died through golden hours,
And the shining moon arising,
How the boat drew homeward filled with flowers!
Bright were your eyes in the night:
We have lived, my love —
O, we have loved, my love.
Frost has bound our flowing river,
Snow has whitened all our island brake,
And beside the winter fagot
Joan and Darby doze and dream and wake.
Still, in the river of dreams,
Swims the boat of love —
Hark! chimes the falling oar!
And again in winter evens
When on firelight dreaming fancy feeds,
In those ears of agèd lovers
Love's own river warbles in the reeds.
Love still the past, O my love!
We have lived of yore,
O, we have loved of yore.

MATER TRIUMPHANS

Son of my woman's body, you go, to the drum and fife,
To taste the colour of love and the other side of life —
From out of the dainty the rude, the strong from out of the frail,
Eternally through the ages from the female comes the male.
The ten fingers and toes, and the shell-like nail on each,
The eyes blind as gems and the tongue attempting speech;
Impotent hands in my bosom, and yet they shall wield the sword!
Drugged with slumber and milk, you wait the day of the Lord.
Infant bridegroom, uncrowned king, unanointed priest,
Soldier, lover, explorer, I see you nuzzle the breast.
You that grope in my bosom shall load the ladies with rings,
You, that came forth through the doors, shall burst the doors of kings.

Bright is the ring of words
When the right man rings them,
Fair the fall of songs
When the singer sings them.

Still they are carolled and said —
On wings they are carried —
After the singer is dead
And the maker buried.
Low as the singer lies
In the field of heather,
Songs of his fashion bring
The swains together.
And when the west is red
With the sunset embers,
The lover lingers and sings
And the maid remembers.

In the highlands, in the country places,
Where the old plain men have rosy faces,
And the young fair maidens
Quiet eyes;
Where essential silence cheers and blesses,
And for ever in the hill-recesses
Her more lovely music
Broods and dies.
O to mount again where erst I haunted;
Where the old red hills are bird-enchanted,
And the low green meadows
Bright with sward;
And when even dies, the million-tinted,
And the night has come, and planets glinted,
Lo, the valley hollow
Lamp-bestarred!

O to dream, O to awake and wander
There, and with delight to take and render,
Through the trance of silence,

Quiet breath;
Lo! for there, among the flowers and grasses,
Only the mightier movement sounds and passes;
Only winds and rivers,
Life and death.

TO THE TUNE OF WANDERING WILLIE

Home no more home to me, whither must I wander?
Hunger my driver, I go where I must.
Cold blows the winter wind over hill and heather;
Thick drives the rain, and my roof is in the dust.
Loved of wise men was the shade of my rooftree,
The true word of welcome was spoken in the door —
Dear days of old, with the faces in the firelight,
Kind folks of old, you come again no more.
Home was home then, my dear, full of kindly faces,
Home was home then, my dear, happy for the child.
Fire and the windows bright glittered on the moorland;
Song, tuneful song, built a palace in the wild.
Now, when day dawns on the brow of the moorland,
Lone stands the house, and the chimney-stone is cold.
Lone let it stand, now the friends are all departed,
The kind hearts, the true hearts, that loved the place of old.
Spring shall come, come again, calling up the moorfowl,
Spring shall bring the sun and rain, bring the bees and flowers;
Red shall the heather bloom over hill and valley,
Soft flow the stream through the even-flowing hours;

Fair the day shine as it shone on my childhood —
Fair shine the day on the house with open door;
Birds come and cry there and twitter in the chimney —
But I go for ever and come again no more.

WINTER

In rigorous hours, when down the iron lane
The redbreast looks in vain
For hips and haws,
Lo, shining flowers upon my window-pane
The silver pencil of the winter draws.
When all the snowy hill
And the bare woods are still;
When snipes are silent in the frozen bogs,
And all the garden garth is whelmed in mire,
Lo, by the hearth, the laughter of the logs —
More fair than roses, lo, the flowers of fire!
Saranac Lake.

The stormy evening closes now in vain,
Loud wails the wind and beats the driving rain,
While here in sheltered house
With fire-ypainted walls,
I hear the wind abroad,
I hark the calling squalls —
"Blow, blow," I cry, "you burst your cheeks in vain!
Blow, blow," I cry, "my love is home again!"

Yon ship you chase perchance but yesternight
Bore still the precious freight of my delight,
That here in sheltered house
With fire-ypainted walls,
Now hears the wind abroad,
Now harks the calling squalls.
"Blow, blow," I cry, "in vain you rouse the sea,
My rescued sailor shares the fire with me!"

TO DR. HAKE

(ON RECEIVING A COPY OF VERSES)

In the belovèd hour that ushers day,
In the pure dew, under the breaking grey,
One bird, ere yet the woodland quires awake,
With brief réveillé summons all the brake:
Chirp, chirp, it goes; nor waits an answer long;
And that small signal fills the grove with song.
Thus on my pipe I breathed a strain or two;
It scarce was music, but 'twas all I knew.
It was not music, for I lacked the art,
Yet what but frozen music filled my heart?
Chirp, chirp, I went, nor hoped a nobler strain;
But Heaven decreed I should not pipe in vain,
For, lo! not far from there, in secret dale,
All silent, sat an ancient nightingale.
My sparrow notes he heard; thereat awoke;
And with a tide of song his silence broke.

TO — —

I knew thee strong and quiet like the hills;
I knew thee apt to pity, brave to endure,
In peace or war a Roman full equipt;
And just I knew thee, like the fabled kings
Who by the loud seashore gave judgment forth,
From dawn to eve, bearded and few of words.
What, what, was I to honour thee? A child;
A youth in ardour but a child in strength,
Who after virtue's golden chariot-wheels
Runs ever panting, nor attains the goal.
So thought I, and was sorrowful at heart.
Since then my steps have visited that flood
Along whose shore the numerous footfalls cease,
The voices and the tears of life expire.
Thither the prints go down, the hero's way
Trod large upon the sand, the trembling maid's:
Nimrod that wound his trumpet in the wood,
And the poor, dreaming child, hunter of flowers,
That here his hunting closes with the great:
So one and all go down, nor aught returns.
For thee, for us, the sacred river waits,
For me, the unworthy, thee, the perfect friend;
There Blame desists, there his unfaltering dogs
He from the chase recalls, and homeward rides;
Yet Praise and Love pass over and go in.
So when, beside that margin, I discard
My more than mortal weakness, and with thee
Through that still land unfearing I advance;
If then at all we keep the touch of joy,
Thou shalt rejoice to find me altered — I,
O Felix, to behold thee still unchanged.

The morning drum-call on my eager ear
Thrills unforgotten yet; the morning dew
Lies yet undried along my field of noon.
But now I pause at whiles in what I do,
And count the bell, and tremble lest I hear
(My work untrimmed) the sunset gun too soon.

I have trod the upward and the downward slope;
I have endured and done in days before;
I have longed for all, and bid farewell to hope;
And I have lived and loved, and closed the door.

He hears with gladdened heart the thunder
Peal, and loves the falling dew;
He knows the earth above and under —
Sits and is content to view.
He sits beside the dying ember,
God for hope and man for friend,

Content to see, glad to remember,
Expectant of the certain end.

Farewell, fair day and fading light!
The clay-born here, with westward sight,
Marks the huge sun now downward soar.
Farewell. We twain shall meet no more.

Farewell. I watch with bursting sigh
My late contemned occasion die.
I linger useless in my tent:
Farewell, fair day, so foully spent!
Farewell, fair day. If any God
At all consider this poor clod,
He who the fair occasion sent
Prepared and placed the impediment.
Let Him diviner vengeance take —
Give me to sleep, give me to wake
Girded and shod, and bid me play
The hero in the coming day!

IF THIS WERE FAITH

God, if this were enough,
That I see things bare to the buff
And up to the buttocks in mire;
That I ask nor hope nor hire,
Nut in the husk,
Nor dawn beyond the dusk,
Nor life beyond death:
God, if this were faith?
Having felt Thy wind in my face
Spit sorrow and disgrace,
Having seen Thine evil doom
In Golgotha and Khartoum,
And the brutes, the work of Thine hands,
Fill with injustice lands
And stain with blood the sea:
If still in my veins the glee

Of the black night and the sun
And the lost battle, run:
If, an adept,
The iniquitous lists I still accept
With joy, and joy to endure and be withstood,
And still to battle and perish for a dream of good:
God, if that were enough?
If to feel in the ink of the slough,
And the sink of the mire,
Veins of glory and fire
Run through and transpierce and transpire,
And a secret purpose of glory in every part,
And the answering glory of battle fill my heart;
To thrill with the joy of girded men,
To go on for ever and fail and go on again,
And be mauled to the earth and arise,
And contend for the shade of a word and a thing not seen with the eyes:
With the half of a broken hope for a pillow at night
That somehow the right is the right
And the smooth shall bloom from the rough:
Lord, if that were enough?

MY WIFE

Trusty, dusky, vivid, true,
With eyes of gold and bramble-dew,
Steel-true and blade-straight,
The great artificer
Made my mate.

Honour, anger, valour, fire;
A love that life could never tire,
Death quench or evil stir,
The mighty master
Gave to her.
Teacher, tender, comrade, wife,
A fellow-farer true through life,
Heart-whole and soul-free
The august father
Gave to me.

TO THE MUSE

Resign the rhapsody, the dream,
To men of larger reach;
Be ours the quest of a plain theme,
The piety of speech.
As monkish scribes from morning break
Toiled till the close of light,
Nor thought a day too long to make
One line or letter bright:
We also with an ardent mind,
Time, wealth, and fame forgot,
Our glory in our patience find
And skim, and skim the pot:
Till last, when round the house we hear
The evensong of birds,
One corner of blue heaven appear
In our clear well of words.

Leave, leave it then, muse of my heart!
Sans finish and sans frame,
Leave unadorned by needless art
The picture as it came.

TO AN ISLAND PRINCESS

Since long ago, a child at home,
I read and longed to rise and roam,
Where'er I went, whate'er I willed,
One promised land my fancy filled.
Hence the long roads my home I made;
Tossed much in ships; have often laid
Below the uncurtained sky my head,
Rain-deluged and wind-buffeted:
And many a thousand hills I crossed
And corners turned — Love's labour lost,
Till, Lady, to your isle of sun
I came not hoping; and, like one
Snatched out of blindness, rubbed my eyes,
And hailed my promised land with cries.
Yes, Lady, here I was at last;
Here found I all I had forecast:
The long roll of the sapphire sea
That keeps the land's virginity;
The stalwart giants of the wood
Laden with toys and flowers and food;
The precious forest pouring out
To compass the whole town about;
The town itself with streets of lawn,
Loved of the moon, blessed by the dawn,
Where the brown children all the day,
Keep up a ceaseless noise of play,

Play in the sun, play in the rain,
Nor ever quarrel or complain; —
And late at night, in the woods of fruit,
Hark I do you hear the passing flute?
I threw one look to either hand,
And knew I was in Fairyland.
And yet one point of being so
I lacked. For, Lady (as you know),
Whoever by his might of hand
Won entrance into Fairyland,
Found always with admiring eyes
A Fairy princess kind and wise.
It was not long I waited; soon
Upon my threshold, in broad noon,
Gracious and helpful, wise and good,
The Fairy Princess Moë stood.
Tantira, Tahiti, *Nov.*

TO KALAKAUA

(WITH A PRESENT OF A PEARL)

The Silver Ship, my King — that was her name
In the bright islands whence your fathers came —
The Silver Ship, at rest from winds and tides,
Below your palace in your harbour rides:
And the seafarers, sitting safe on shore,
Like eager merchants count their treasures o'er.

One gift they find, one strange and lovely thing,
Now doubly precious since it pleased a king.
The right, my liege, is ancient as the lyre
For bards to give to kings what kings admire.
'Tis mine to offer for Apollo's sake;
And since the gift is fitting, yours to take.
To golden hands the golden pearl I bring:
The ocean jewel to the island king.
Honolulu, *Feb.*

TO PRINCESS KAIULANI

[Written in April to Kaiulani in the April of her age; and at Waikiki, within easy walk of Kaiulani's banyan! When she comes to my land and her father's, and the rain beats upon the window (as I fear it will), let her look at this page; it will be like a weed gathered and pressed at home; and she will remember her own islands, and the shadow of the mighty tree; and she will hear the peacocks screaming in the dusk and the wind blowing in the palms; and she will think of her father sitting there alone. — R. L. S.]

>Forth from her land to mine she goes,
>The island maid, the island rose,
>Light of heart and bright of face:
>The daughter of a double race.
>Her islands here, in Southern sun,
>Shall mourn their Kaiulani gone,
>And I, in her dear banyan shade,
>Look vainly for my little maid.
>But our Scots islands far away
>Shall glitter with unwonted day,
>And cast for once their tempests by
>To smile in Kaiulani's eye.
>Honolulu.

TO MOTHER MARYANNE

To see the infinite pity of this place,
The mangled limb, the devastated face,
The innocent sufferer smiling at the rod —
A fool were tempted to deny his God.
He sees, he shrinks. But if he gaze again,
Lo, beauty springing from the breast of pain;
He marks the sisters on the mournful shores;
And even a fool is silent and adores.
Guest House, Kalawao, Molokai.

IN MEMORIAM E.H.

I knew a silver head was bright beyond compare,
I knew a queen of toil with a crown of silver hair.
Garland of valour and sorrow, of beauty and renown,
Life, that honours the brave, crowned her himself with the crown.
The beauties of youth are frail, but this was a jewel of age.
Life, that delights in the brave, gave it himself for a gage.
Fair was the crown to behold, and beauty its poorest part —
At once the scar of the wound and the order pinned on the heart.
The beauties of man are frail, and the silver lies in the dust,
And the queen that we call to mind sleeps with the brave and the just;

Sleeps with the weary at length; but, honoured and ever fair,
Shines in the eye of the mind the crown of the silver hair.
Honolulu.

TO MY WIFE

(A FRAGMENT)

Long must elapse ere you behold again
Green forest frame the entry of the lane —
The wild lane with the bramble and the briar,
The year-old cart-tracks perfect in the mire,
The wayside smoke, perchance, the dwarfish huts,
And ramblers' donkey drinking from the ruts: —
Long ere you trace how deviously it leads,
Back from man's chimneys and the bleating meads
To the woodland shadow, to the silvan hush,
When but the brooklet chuckles in the brush —
Back from the sun and bustle of the vale
To where the great voice of the nightingale
Fills all the forest like a single room,
And all the banks smell of the golden broom;
So wander on until the eve descends,
And back returning to your firelit friends,
You see the rosy sun, despoiled of light,
Hung, caught in thickets, like a schoolboy's kite.
Here from the sea the unfruitful sun shall rise,
Bathe the bare deck and blind the unshielded eyes;
The allotted hours aloft shall wheel in vain
And in the unpregnant ocean plunge again.
Assault of squalls that mock the watchful guard,
And pluck the bursting canvas from the yard,

And senseless clamour of the calm, at night
Must mar your slumbers. By the plunging light,
In beetle-haunted, most unwomanly bower
Of the wild-swerving cabin, hour by hour....
Schooner *Equator*.

TO MY OLD FAMILIARS

Do you remember — can we e'er forget? —
How, in the coiled perplexities of youth,
In our wild climate, in our scowling town,
We gloomed and shivered, sorrowed, sobbed and feared?
The belching winter wind, the missile rain,
The rare and welcome silence of the snows,
The laggard morn, the haggard day, the night,
The grimy spell of the nocturnal town,
Do you remember? — Ah, could one forget!
As when the fevered sick that all night long
Listed the wind intone, and hear at last
The ever-welcome voice of chanticleer
Sing in the bitter hour before the dawn, —
With sudden ardour, these desire the day:
So sang in the gloom of youth the bird of hope;
So we, exulting, hearkened and desired.
For lo! as in the palace porch of life
We huddled with chimeras, from within —
How sweet to hear! — the music swelled and fell,
And through the breach of the revolving doors
What dreams of splendour blinded us and fled!
I have since then contended and rejoiced;
Amid the glories of the house of life
Profoundly entered, and the shrine beheld:
Yet when the lamp from my expiring eyes

Shall dwindle and recede, the voice of love
Fall insignificant on my closing ears,
What sound shall come but the old cry of the wind
In our inclement city? what return
But the image of the emptiness of youth,
Filled with the sound of footsteps and that voice
Of discontent and rapture and despair?
So, as in darkness, from the magic lamp,
The momentary pictures gleam and fade
And perish, and the night resurges — these
Shall I remember, and then all forget.
Apemama.

The tropics vanish, and meseems that I,
From Halkerside, from topmost Allermuir,
Or steep Caerketton, dreaming gaze again.
Far set in fields and woods, the town I see
Spring gallant from the shallows of her smoke,
Cragged, spired, and turreted, her virgin fort
Beflagged. About, on seaward-drooping hills,
New folds of city glitter. Last, the Forth
Wheels ample waters set with sacred isles,
And populous Fife smokes with a score of towns.
There, on the sunny frontage of a hill,

Hard by the house of kings, repose the dead,
My dead, the ready and the strong of word.
Their works, the salt-encrusted, still survive;
The sea bombards their founded towers; the night
Thrills pierced with their strong lamps. The artificers,
One after one, here in this grated cell,
Where the rain erases and the rust consumes,
Fell upon lasting silence. Continents
And continental oceans intervene;

A sea uncharted, on a lampless isle,
Environs and confines their wandering child
In vain. The voice of generations dead
Summons me, sitting distant, to arise,
My numerous footsteps nimbly to retrace,
And, all mutation over, stretch me down
In that denoted city of the dead.
Apemama.

TO S. C.

I heard the pulse of the besieging sea
Throb far away all night. I heard the wind
Fly crying and convulse tumultuous palms.
I rose and strolled. The isle was all bright sand,
And flailing fans and shadows of the palm;
The heaven all moon and wind and the blind vault;
The keenest planet slain, for Venus slept.
The king, my neighbour, with his host of wives,
Slept in the precinct of the palisade;
Where single, in the wind, under the moon,
Among the slumbering cabins, blazed a fire,
Sole street-lamp and the only sentinel.
To other lands and nights my fancy turned —
To London first, and chiefly to your house,
The many-pillared and the well-beloved.
There yearning fancy lighted; there again
In the upper room I lay, and heard far off
The unsleeping city murmur like a shell;
The muffled tramp of the Museum guard
Once more went by me; I beheld again
Lamps vainly brighten the dispeopled street;
Again I longed for the returning morn,
The awaking traffic, the bestirring birds,
The consentaneous trill of tiny song

That weaves round monumental cornices
A passing charm of beauty. Most of all,
For your light foot I wearied, and your knock
That was the glad réveillé of my day.
Lo, now, when to your task in the great house
At morning through the portico you pass,
One moment glance, where by the pillared wall
Far-voyaging island gods, begrimed with smoke,
Sit now unworshipped, the rude monument
Of faiths forgot and races undivined;
Sit now disconsolate, remembering well
The priest, the victim, and the songful crowd,
The blaze of the blue noon, and that huge voice,
Incessant, of the breakers on the shore.
As far as these from their ancestral shrine,
So far, so foreign, your divided friends
Wander, estranged in body, not in mind.
Apemama.

THE HOUSE OF TEMBINOKA

[At my departure from the island of Apemama, for which you will look in vain in most atlases, the King and I agreed, since we both set up to be in the poetical way, that we should celebrate our separation in verse. Whether or not his Majesty has been true to his bargain, the laggard posts of the Pacific may perhaps inform me in six months, perhaps not before a year. The following lines represent my part of the contract, and it is hoped, by their pictures of strange manners, they may entertain a civilised audience. Nothing throughout has been invented or exaggerated; the lady herein referred to as the author's muse has confined herself to stringing into rhyme facts or legends that I saw or heard during two months' residence upon the island. — R. L. S.]

ENVOI
Let us, who part like brothers, part like bards;
And you in your tongue and measure, I in mine,
Our now division duly solemnise.
Unlike the strains, and yet the theme is one:

The strains unlike, and how unlike their fate!
You to the blinding palace-yard shall call
The prefect of the singers, and to him,
Listening devout, your valedictory verse
Deliver; he, his attribute fulfilled,
To the island chorus hand your measures on,
Wed now with harmony: so them, at last,
Night after night, in the open hall of dance,
Shall thirty matted men, to the clapped hand,
Intone and bray and bark. Unfortunate!
Paper and print alone shall honour mine.

THE SONG

Let now the King his ear arouse
And toss the bosky ringlets from his brows,
The while, our bond to implement,
My muse relates and praises his descent.

I

Bride of the shark, her valour first I sing
Who on the lone seas quickened of a King.
She, from the shore and puny homes of men,
Beyond the climber's sea-discerning ken,
Swam, led by omens; and devoid of fear,
Beheld her monstrous paramour draw near.
She gazed; all round her to the heavenly pale,
The simple sea was void of isle or sail —
Sole overhead the unsparing sun was reared —
When the deep bubbled and the brute appeared.
But she, secure in the decrees of fate,
Made strong her bosom and received the mate,

And, men declare, from that marine embrace
Conceived the virtues of a stronger race.

II

Her stern descendant next I praise,
Survivor of a thousand frays: —
In the hall of tongues who ruled the throng;
Led and was trusted by the strong;
And when spears were in the wood,
Like a tower of vantage stood: —
Whom, not till seventy years had sped,
Unscarred of breast, erect of head,
Still light of step, still bright of look,
The hunter, Death, had overtook.

III

His sons, the brothers twain, I sing.
Of whom the elder reigned a King.
No Childeric he, yet much declined
From his rude sire's imperious mind,
Until his day came when he died,
He lived, he reigned, he versified.
But chiefly him I celebrate
That was the pillar of the state,
Ruled, wise of word and bold of mien,
The peaceful and the warlike scene;
And played alike the leader's part
In lawful and unlawful art.
His soldiers with emboldened ears
Heard him laugh among the spears.
He could deduce from age to age

The web of island parentage;
Best lay the rhyme, best lead the dance,
For any festal circumstance:

And fitly fashion oar and boat,
A palace or an armour coat.
None more availed than he to raise
The strong, suffumigating blaze,
Or knot the wizard leaf: none more,
Upon the untrodden windward shore
Of the isle, beside the beating main,
To cure the sickly and constrain,
With muttered words and waving rods,
The gibbering and the whistling gods.
But he, though thus with hand and head
He ruled, commanded, charmed, and led,
And thus in virtue and in might
Towered to contemporary sight —
Still in fraternal faith and love,
Remained below to reach above,
Gave and obeyed the apt command,
Pilot and vassal of the land.

IV

My Tembinok' from men like these
Inherited his palaces,
His right to rule, his powers of mind,
His cocoa-islands sea-enshrined.
Stern bearer of the sword and whip,
A master passed in mastership,
He learned, without the spur of need,
To write, to cipher, and to read;
From all that touch on his prone shore
Augments his treasury of lore,
Eager in age as erst in youth
To catch an art, to learn a truth,
To paint on the internal page
A clearer picture of the age.

His age, you say? But ah, not so!
In his lone isle of long ago,
A royal Lady of Shalott,
Sea-sundered, he beholds it not;
He only hears it far away.
The stress of equatorial day
He suffers; he records the while
The vapid annals of the isle;
Slaves bring him praise of his renown,
Or cackle of the palm-tree town;
The rarer ship and the rare boat
He marks; and only hears remote,
Where thrones and fortunes rise and reel,
The thunder of the turning wheel.

V

For the unexpected tears he shed
At my departing, may his lion head
Not whiten, his revolving years
No fresh occasion minister of tears;
At book or cards, at work or sport,
Him may the breeze across the palace court
For ever fan; and swelling near
For ever the loud song divert his ear.

Schooner *Equator*, at Sea.

THE WOODMAN

In all the grove, nor stream nor bird
Nor aught beside my blows was heard,
And the woods wore their noonday dress —
The glory of their silentness.

From the island summit to the seas,
Trees mounted, and trees drooped, and trees
Groped upward in the gaps. The green
Inarboured talus and ravine
By fathoms. By the multitude,
The rugged columns of the wood
And bunches of the branches stood:
Thick as a mob, deep as a sea,
And silent as eternity.
With lowered axe, with backward head,
Late from this scene my labourer fled,
And with a ravelled tale to tell,
Returned. Some denizen of hell,
Dead man or disinvested god,
Had close behind him peered and trod,
And triumphed when he turned to flee.
How different fell the lines with me!
Whose eye explored the dim arcade
Impatient of the uncoming shade —
Shy elf, or dryad pale and cold,
Or mystic lingerer from of old:
Vainly. The fair and stately things,
Impassive as departed kings,
All still in the wood's stillness stood,
And dumb. The rooted multitude
Nodded and brooded, bloomed and dreamed,
Unmeaning, undivined. It seemed
No other art, no hope, they knew,
Than clutch the earth and seek the blue.
'Mid vegetable king and priest
And stripling, I (the only beast)
Was at the beast's work, killing; hewed
The stubborn roots across, bestrewed
The glebe with the dislustred leaves,
And bade the saplings fall in sheaves;

Bursting across the tangled math
A ruin that I called a path,
A Golgotha that, later on,
When rains had watered, and suns shone,
And seeds enriched the place, should bear
And be called garden. Here and there,
I spied and plucked by the green hair
A foe more resolute to live,
The toothed and killing sensitive.

He, semi-conscious, fled the attack;
He shrank and tucked his branches back;
And straining by his anchor strand,
Captured and scratched the rooting hand.
I saw him crouch, I felt him bite;
And straight my eyes were touched with sight.
I saw the wood for what it was;
The lost and the victorious cause;
The deadly battle pitched in line,
Saw silent weapons cross and shine:
Silent defeat, silent assault,
A battle and a burial vault.
Thick round me in the teeming mud
Briar and fern strove to the blood.
The hooked liana in his gin
Noosed his reluctant neighbours in:
There the green murderer throve and spread,
Upon his smothering victims fed,
And wantoned on his climbing coil.
Contending roots fought for the soil
Like frightened demons: with despair
Competing branches pushed for air.
Green conquerors from overhead
Bestrode the bodies of their dead;
The Caesars of the silvan field,
Unused to fail, foredoomed to yield:

For in the groins of branches, lo!
The cancers of the orchid grow.
Silent as in the listed ring
Two chartered wrestlers strain and cling,
Dumb as by yellow Hooghly's side
The suffocating captives died:
So hushed the woodland warfare goes
Unceasing; and the silent foes
Grapple and smother, strain and clasp
Without a cry, without a gasp.
Here also sound Thy fans, O God,
Here too Thy banners move abroad:
Forest and city, sea and shore,
And the whole earth, Thy threshing-floor!
The drums of war, the drums of peace,
Roll through our cities without cease,
And all the iron halls of life
Ring with the unremitting strife.
The common lot we scarce perceive.
Crowds perish, we nor mark nor grieve:
The bugle calls — we mourn a few!
What corporal's guard at Waterloo?
What scanty hundreds more or less
In the man-devouring Wilderness?
What handful bled on Delhi ridge?
— See, rather, London, on thy bridge

The pale battalions trample by,
Resolved to slay, resigned to die.
Count, rather, all the maimed and dead
In the unbrotherly war of bread.
See, rather, under sultrier skies
What vegetable Londons rise,
And teem, and suffer without sound.
Or in your tranquil garden ground,
Contented, in the falling gloom,
Saunter and see the roses bloom.

That these might live, what thousands died!
All day the cruel hoe was plied;
The ambulance barrow rolled all day;
Your wife, the tender, kind, and gay,
Donned her long gauntlets, caught the spud
And bathed in vegetable blood;
And the long massacre now at end,
See! where the lazy coils ascend,
See, where the bonfire sputters red
At even, for the innocent dead.
Why prate of peace? when, warriors all,
We clank in harness into hall,
And ever bare upon the board
Lies the necessary sword.
In the green field or quiet street,
Besieged we sleep, beleaguered eat;
Labour by day and wake o' nights,
In war with rival appetites.
The rose on roses feeds; the lark
On larks. The sedentary clerk
All morning with a diligent pen
Murders the babes of other men;
And like the beasts of wood and park,
Protects his whelps, defends his den.
Unshamed the narrow aim I hold;
I feed my sheep, patrol my fold;
Breathe war on wolves and rival flocks,
A pious outlaw on the rocks
Of God and morning; and when time
Shall bow, or rivals break me, climb
Where no undubbed civilian dares,
In my war harness, the loud stairs
Of honour; and my conqueror
Hail me a warrior fallen in war.
Vailima.

TROPIC RAIN

As the single pang of the blow, when the metal is mingled well,
Rings and lives and resounds in all the bounds of the bell,
So the thunder above spoke with a single tongue,
So in the heart of the mountain the sound of it rumbled and clung.
Sudden the thunder was drowned — quenched was the levin light —
And the angel-spirit of rain laughed out loud in the night.
Loud as the maddened river raves in the cloven glen,
Angel of rain! you laughed and leaped on the roofs of men;
And the sleepers sprang in their beds, and joyed and feared as you fell.
You struck, and my cabin quailed; the roof of it roared like a bell.
You spoke, and at once the mountain shouted and shook with brooks.
You ceased, and the day returned, rosy, with virgin looks.
And methought that beauty and terror are only one, not two;
And the world has room for love, and death, and thunder, and dew;
And all the sinews of hell slumber in summer air;
And the face of God is a rock, but the face of the rock is fair.

Beneficent streams of tears flow at the finger of pain;
And out of the cloud that smites, beneficent rivers of rain.
Vailima.

AN END OF TRAVEL

Let now your soul in this substantial world
Some anchor strike. Be here the body moored; —
This spectacle immutably from now
The picture in your eye; and when time strikes,
And the green scene goes on the instant blind —
The ultimate helpers, where your horse to-day
Conveyed you dreaming, bear your body dead.
Vailima.

We uncommiserate pass into the night
From the loud banquet, and departing leave
A tremor in men's memories, faint and sweet
And frail as music. Features of our face,
The tones of the voice, the touch of the loved hand,
Perish and vanish, one by one, from earth:
Meanwhile, in the hall of song, the multitude
Applauds the new performer. One, perchance,
One ultimate survivor lingers on,
And smiles, and to his ancient heart recalls
The long forgotten. Ere the morrow die,
He too, returning, through the curtain comes,
And the new age forgets us and goes on.

Sing me a song of a lad that is gone,
Say, could that lad be I?
Merry of soul he sailed on a day
Over the sea to Skye.
Mull was astern, Rum on the port,
Eigg on the starboard bow;
Glory of youth glowed in his soul:
Where is that glory now?
Sing me a song of a lad that is gone,
Say, could that lad be I?
Merry of soul he sailed on a day
Over the sea to Skye.
Give me again all that was there,
Give me the sun that shone!
Give me the eyes, give me the soul,
Give me the lad that's gone!
Sing me a song of a lad that is gone,
Say, could that lad be I?
Merry of soul he sailed on a day
Over the sea to Skye.
Billow and breeze, islands and seas,
Mountains of rain and sun,
All that was good, all that was fair,
All that was me is gone.

TO S.R. CROCKETT

(ON RECEIVING A DEDICATION)

Blows the wind to-day, and the sun and the rain are flying,
Blows the wind on the moors to-day and now,
Where about the graves of the martyrs the whaups are crying,
My heart remembers how!
Grey recumbent tombs of the dead in desert places,
Standing-stones on the vacant wine-red moor,
Hills of sheep, and the homes of the silent vanished races,
And winds, austere and pure:
Be it granted me to behold you again in dying,
Hills of home! and to hear again the call;
Hear about the graves of the martyrs the peewees crying,
And hear no more at all.
Vailima.

EVENSONG

The embers of the day are red
Beyond the murky hill.
The kitchen smokes: the bed
In the darkling house is spread:
The great sky darkens overhead,

And the great woods are shrill.
So far have I been led,
Lord, by Thy will:
So far I have followed, Lord, and wondered still.
The breeze from the embalmèd land
Blows sudden toward the shore,
And claps my cottage door.
I hear the signal, Lord — I understand.
The night at Thy command
Comes. I will eat and sleep and will not question more.
Vailima.

THE LESSON OF THE MASTER

TO HENRY JAMES

Adela, Adela, Adela Chart,
What have you done to my elderly heart?
Of all the ladies of paper and ink
I count you the paragon, call you the pink.
The word of your brother depicts you in part:
"You raving maniac!" Adela Chart;
But in all the asylums that cumber the ground,
So delightful a maniac was ne'er to be found.
I pore on you, dote on you, clasp you to heart,
I laud, love, and laugh at you, Adela Chart,
And thank my dear maker the while I admire
That I can be neither your husband nor sire.
Your husband's, your sire's, were a difficult part;
You're a byway to suicide, Adela Chart;
But to read of, depicted by exquisite James,
O, sure you're the flower and quintessence of dames.

Vailima, *October*.

A FAMILIAR EPISTLE

Blame me not that this epistle
Is the first you have from me;
Idleness hath held me fettered;
But at last the times are bettered,
And once more I wet my whistle
Here in France beside the sea.
All the green and idle weather,
I have had in sun and shower
Such an easy, warm subsistence,
Such an indolent existence,
I should find it hard to sever
Day from day and hour from hour.
Many a tract-provided ranter
May upbraid me, dark and sour,
Many a bland Utilitarian,
Or excited Millenarian,
— "*Pereunt et imputantur*" —
You must speak to every hour.
But (the very term's deception)
You at least, my Friend, will see
That in sunny grassy meadows,
Trailed across by moving shadows,
To be actively receptive
Is as much as man can be.

He that all the winter grapples
Difficulties — thrust and ward —
Needs to cheer him thro' his duty
Memories of sun and beauty,
Orchards with the russet apples
Lying scattered on the sward.
Many such I keep in prison,
Keep them here at heart unseen,
Till my muse again rehearses
Long years hence, and in my verses
You shall meet them rearisen,
Ever comely, ever green.
You know how they never perish,
How, in time of later art,
Memories consecrate and sweeten
Those defaced and tempest-beaten
Flowers of former years we cherish
Half a life, against our heart.
Most, those love-fruits withered greenly,
Those frail, sickly amourettes, —
How they brighten with the distance,
Take new strength and new existence,
Till we see them sitting queenly
Crowned and courted by regrets!

All that loveliest and best is,
Aureole-fashion round their head,
They that looked in life but plainly,
How they stir our spirits vainly
When they come to us, Alcestis —
Like returning from the dead!

Not the old love but another,
Bright she comes at memory's call,
Our forgotten vows reviving
To a newer, livelier living,
As the dead child to the mother
Seems the fairest child of all.
Thus our Goethe, sacred master,
Travelling backward thro' his youth,
Surely wandered wrong in trying
To renew the old, undying
Loves that cling in memory faster
Than they ever lived in truth.
Boulogne-sur-Mer, *September.*

EPISTLE TO CHARLES BAXTER

Noo lyart leaves blaw ower the green,
Red are the bonny woods o' Dean,
An' here we're back in Embro, freen',
To pass the winter.
Whilk noo, wi' frosts afore, draws in,
An' snaws ahint her.
I've seen 's hae days to fricht us a',
The Pentlands poothered weel wi' snaw,
The ways half-smoored wi' liquid thaw,
An' half-congealin',
The snell an' scowtherin' norther blaw
Frae blae Brunteelan'.

I've seen 's been unco sweir to sally,
And at the door-cheeks daff an' dally,
Seen 's daidle thus an' shilly-shally
For near a minute —
Sae cauld the wind blew up the valley,
The deil was in it! —
Syne spread the silk an' tak the gate,
In blast an' blaudin', rain, deil hae 't!
The hale toon glintin', stane an' slate,
Wi' cauld an' weet,
An' to the Court, gin we 'se be late,
Bicker oor feet.
And at the Court, tae, aft I saw
Whaur Advocates by twa an' twa
Gang gesterin' end to end the ha'
In weeg an' goon,
To crack o' what ye wull but Law
The hale forenoon.
That muckle ha', maist like a kirk,
I've kent at braid mid-day sae mirk
Ye'd seen white weegs an' faces lurk
Like ghaists frae Hell,
But whether Christian ghaists or Turk,
Deil ane could tell.
The three fires lunted in the gloom,
The wind blew like the blast o' doom,
The rain upo' the roof abune
Played Peter Dick —
Ye wad nae'd licht enough i' the room
Your teeth to pick!

But, freend, ye ken how me an' you,
The ling-lang lanely winter through,
Keep'd a guid speerit up, an' true
To lore Horatian,
We aye the ither bottle drew
To inclination.

Sae let us in the comin' days
Stand sicker on our auncient ways —
The strauchtest road in a' the maze
Since Eve ate apples;
An' let the winter weet our cla'es —
We'll weet oor thrapples.
Edinburgh, *October.*

EPISTLE TO ALBERT DEW-SMITH

Figure me to yourself, I pray —
A man of my peculiar cut —
Apart from dancing and deray,
Into an Alpine valley shut;
Shut in a kind of damned Hotel,
Discountenanced by God and man;
The food? — Sir, you would do as well
To cram your belly full of bran.
The company? Alas, the day
That I should dwell with such a crew,
With devil anything to say,
Nor any one to say it to!
The place? Although they call it Platz,
I will be bold and state my view;
It's not a place at all — and that's
The bottom verity, my Dew.

There are, as I will not deny,
Innumerable inns; a road;
Several Alps indifferent high;
The snow's inviolable abode;
Eleven English parsons, all
Entirely inoffensive; four
True human beings — what I call
Human — the deuce a cipher more;
A climate of surprising worth;
Innumerable dogs that bark;
Some air, some weather, and some earth;
A native race — God save the mark! —
A race that works, yet cannot work,
Yodels, but cannot yodel right,
Such as, unhelp'd, with rusty dirk,
I vow that I could wholly smite.
A river that from morn to night
Down all the valley plays the fool;
Not once she pauses in her flight,
Nor knows the comfort of a pool;
But still keeps up, by straight or bend,
The selfsame pace she hath begun —
Still hurry, hurry, to the end —
Good God, is that the way to run?
If I a river were, I hope
That I should better realise
The opportunities and scope
Of that romantic enterprise.

I should not ape the merely strange,
But aim besides at the divine;
And continuity and change
I still should labour to combine.

Here should I gallop down the race,
Here charge the sterling like a bull;
There, as a man might wipe his face,
Lie, pleased and panting, in a pool.
But what, my Dew, in idle mood,
What prate I, minding not my debt?
What do I talk of bad or good?
The best is still a cigarette.
Me whether evil fate assault,
Or smiling providences crown —
Whether on high the eternal vault
Be blue, or crash with thunder down —
I judge the best, whate'er befall,
Is still to sit on one's behind,
And, having duly moistened all,
Smoke with an unperturbed mind.
Davos, *November*.

RONDELS

Far have you come, my lady, from the town,
And far from all your sorrows, if you please,
To smell the good sea-winds and hear the seas,
And in green meadows lay your body down.
To find your pale face grow from pale to brown,
Your sad eyes growing brighter by degrees;
Far have you come, my lady, from the town,
And far from all your sorrows, if you please.
Here in this seaboard land of old renown,
In meadow grass go wading to the knees;
Bathe your whole soul a while in simple ease;
There is no sorrow but the sea can drown;
Far have you come, my lady, from the town.

Nous n'irons plus au bois
We'll walk the woods no more,
But stay beside the fire,
To weep for old desire
And things that are no more.
The woods are spoiled and hoar,
The ways are full of mire;
We'll walk the woods no more,
But stay beside the fire.
We loved, in days of yore,
Love, laughter, and the lyre.
Ah God, but death is dire,
And death is at the door —
We'll walk the woods no more.
Château Renard, *August*.

Since I am sworn to live my life
And not to keep an easy heart,
Some men may sit and drink apart,
I bear a banner in the strife.
Some can take quiet thought to wife,
I am all day at *tierce* and *carte*,
Since I am sworn to live my life
And not to keep an easy heart.
I follow gaily to the fife,
Leave Wisdom bowed above a chart,
And Prudence brawing in the mart,
And dare Misfortune to the knife,
Since I am sworn to live my life.

OF HIS PITIABLE TRANSFORMATION

I who was young so long,
Young and alert and gay,
Now that my hair is grey,
Begin to change my song.
Now I know right from wrong,
Now I know *pay* and *pray*,
I who was young so long,
Young and alert and gay.
Now I follow the throng,
Walk in the beaten way,
Hear what the elders say,
And own that I was wrong —
I who was young so long.

THE SUSQUEHANNAH AND THE DELAWARE

Of where or how, I nothing know;
And why, I do not care;
Enough if, even so,
My travelling eyes, my travelling mind can go
By flood and field and hill, by wood and meadow fair,
Beside the Susquehannah and along the Delaware.
I think, I hope, I dream no more
The dreams of otherwhere,
The cherished thoughts of yore;
I have been changed from what I was before;
And drunk too deep perchance the lotus of the air,
Beside the Susquehannah and along the Delaware.

Unweary, God me yet shall bring
To lands of brighter air,
Where I, now half a king,
Shall with enfranchised spirit loudlier sing,
And wear a bolder front than that which now I wear
Beside the Susquehannah and along the Delaware.
August.

ALCAICS TO HORATIO F. BROWN

Brave lads in olden musical centuries,
Sang, night by night, adorable choruses,
Sat late by alehouse doors in April
Chaunting in joy as the moon was rising:

Moon-seen and merry, under the trellises,
Flush-faced they played with old polysyllables;
Spring scents inspired, old wine diluted;
Love and Apollo were there to chorus.

Now these, the songs, remain to eternity,
Those, only those, the bountiful choristers
Gone — those are gone, those unremembered
Sleep and are silent in earth for ever.

So man himself appears and evanishes,
So smiles and goes; as wanderers halting at
Some green-embowered house, play their music,
Play and are gone on the windy highway;

Yet dwells the strain enshrined in the memory
Long after they departed eternally,
Forth-faring tow'rd far mountain summits,
Cities of men on the sounding Ocean.

Youth sang the song in years immemorial;
Brave chanticleer, he sang and was beautiful;
Bird-haunted, green treetops in springtime
Heard and were pleased by the voice of singing;

Youth goes, and leaves behind him a prodigy —
Songs sent by thee afar from Venetian
Sea-grey lagunes, sea-paven highways,
Dear to me here in my Alpine exile.

Davos, *Spring*.

A LYTLE JAPE OF TUSHERIE

By A. Tusher

The pleasant river gushes
Among the meadows green;
At home the author tushes;
For him it flows unseen.
The Birds among the Bushes
May wanton on the spray;
But vain for him who tushes
The brightness of the day!
The frog among the rushes
Sits singing in the blue.
By 'r la'kin! but these tushes
Are wearisome to do!
The task entirely crushes
The spirit of the bard:
God pity him who tushes —
His task is very hard.
The filthy gutter slushes,
The clouds are full of rain,
But doomed is he who tushes
To tush and tush again.
At morn with his hair-brushes,
Still "tush" he says and weeps;
At night again he tushes,
And tushes till he sleeps.

And when at length he pushes
Beyond the river dark —
'Las, to the man who tushes,
"Tush" shall be God's remark!
Hyères, *May.*

TO VIRGIL AND DORA WILLIAMS

Here, from the forelands of the tideless sea,
Behold and take my offering unadorned.
In the Pacific air it sprang; it grew
Among the silence of the Alpine air;
In Scottish heather blossomed; and at last
By that unshapen sapphire, in whose face
Spain, Italy, France, Algiers, and Tunis view
Their introverted mountains, came to fruit.
Back now, my Booklet! on the diving ship,
And posting on the rails, to home return, —
Home, and the friends whose honouring name you bear.
Hyères.

BURLESQUE SONNET

TO ÆNEAS WILLIAM MACKINTOSH

Thee, Mackintosh, artificer of light,
Thee, the lone smoker hails! the student, thee;
Thee, oft upon the ungovernable sea,
The seaman, conscious of approaching night;
Thou, with industrious fingers, hast outright
Mastered that art, of other arts the key,
That bids thick night before the morning flee,
And lingering day retains for mortal sight.

O Promethean workman, thee I hail,
Thee hallowed, thee unparalleled, thee bold
To affront the reign of sleep and darkness old,
Thee William, thee Æneas, thee I sing;
Thee by the glimmering taper clear and pale,
Of light, and light's purveyance, hail, the king.

THE FINE PACIFIC ISLANDS

(HEARD IN A PUBLIC-HOUSE AT ROTHERHITHE)

The jolly English Yellowboy
Is a 'ansome coin when new,
The Yankee Double-eagle
Is large enough for two.
O, these may do for seaport towns,
For cities these may do;
But the dibbs that takes the Hislands
Are the dollars of Peru:
O, the fine Pacific Hislands,
O, the dollars of Peru!
It's there we buy the cocoanuts
Mast 'eaded in the blue;
It's there we trap the lasses
All waiting for the crew;
It's there we buy the trader's rum
What bores a seaman through....
In the fine Pacific Hislands
With the dollars of Peru:
In the fine Pacific Hislands
With the dollars of Peru!

Now, messmates, when my watch is up,
And I am quite broached to,
I'll give a tip to 'Evving
Of the 'ansome thing to do:
Let 'em just refit this sailor-man
And launch him off anew
To cruise among the Hislands
With the dollars of Peru:
In the fine Pacific Hislands
With the dollars of Peru!
Tahiti, *August.*

AULD REEKIE

When chitterin' cauld the day sall daw,
Loud may your bonny bugles blaw
And loud your drums may beat.
Hie owre the land at evenfa'
Your lamps may glitter raw by raw,
Along the gowsty street.
I gang nae mair where ance I gaed,
By Brunston, Fairmileheid, or Braid;
But far frae Kirk and Tron.
O still ayont the muckle sea,
Still are ye dear, and dear to me,
Auld Reekie, still and on!

THE CONSECRATION OF BRAILLE

TO MRS A. BAKER

I was a barren tree before,
I blew a quenchèd coal,
I could not, on their midnight shore,
The lonely blind console.

A moment, lend your hand, I bring
My sheaf for you to bind,
And you can teach my words to sing
In the darkness of the blind.
Vailima, *December.*

SONG

Light foot and tight foot,
And green grass spread,
Early in the morning,
But hope is on ahead.
Brief day and bright day,
And sunset red,
Early in the evening,
The stars are overhead.

THE LIGHTKEEPER

I

The brilliant kernel of the night,
The flaming lightroom circles me:
I sit within a blaze of light
Held high above the dusky sea.
Far off the surf doth break and roar
Along bleak miles of moonlit shore,
Where through the tides the tumbling wave
Falls in an avalanche of foam
And drives its churnèd waters home
Up many an undercliff and cave.
The clear bell chimes: the clockworks strain:
The turning lenses flash and pass,
Frame turning within glittering frame
With frosty gleam of moving glass:
Unseen by me, each dusky hour
The sea-waves welter up the tower
Or in the ebb subside again;
And ever and anon all night,
Drawn from afar by charm of light,
A seabird beats against the pane.
And lastly when dawn ends the night
And belts the semi-orb of sea,
The tall, pale pharos in the light
Looks white and spectral as may be.

The early ebb is out: the green
Straight belt of seaweed now is seen,
That round the basement of the tower
Marks out the interspace of tide;
And watching men are heavy-eyed,
And sleepless lips are dry and sour.
The night is over like a dream:
The seabirds cry and dip themselves;
And in the early sunlight, steam
The newly-bared and dripping shelves,
Around whose verge the glassy wave
With lisping wash is heard to lave;
While, on the white tower lifted high,
With yellow light in faded glass
The circling lenses flash and pass,
And sickly shine against the sky.
1869.

II

As the steady lenses circle
With a frosty gleam of glass;
And the clear bell chimes,
And the oil brims over the lip of the burner,

Quiet and still at his desk,
The lonely lightkeeper
Holds his vigil.
Lured from afar,
The bewildered seagull beats
Dully against the lantern;
Yet he stirs not, lifts not his head
From the desk where he reads,
Lifts not his eyes to see
The chill blind circle of night
Watching him through the panes.

This is his country's guardian,
The outmost sentry of peace.
This is the man,
Who gives up all that is lovely in living
For the means to live.
Poetry cunningly gilds
The life of the LightKeeper,
Held on high in the blackness
In the burning kernel of night.
The seaman sees and blesses him;
The Poet, deep in a sonnet,
Numbers his inky fingers
Fitly to praise him:
Only we behold him,
Sitting, patient and stolid,
Martyr to a salary.
1870.

www.ingramcontent.com/pod-product-compliance
Lightning Source LLC
LaVergne TN
LVHW011928070526
838202LV00054B/4541